Tarot for Beginners:

The Most Comprehensive Guide to Tarot Cards Reading, Psychic Tarot Reading, Art of Tarot, Major Arcana, Tarot Card Meanings, Great to Listen in a Car!

Table of Contents

Introduction..9

Chapter 1: The History of the Tarot........................11

    The Debate of the Origins

Chapter 2: Learning the Art of Tarot......................17

    Connecting with your Intuition
    Choosing Your Deck
    The Different Types of Deck

Chapter 3: How to Read the Tarot Cards...............24

    Decision-Making
    Quality of Life
    Insight and Life Help
    Helping Others Around You

Chapter 4: The Major Arcana..................................29

    The Magician
    The High Priestess
    The Empress
    The Emperor
    The Hierophant
    The Lovers
    The Chariot
    Strength
    The Hermit

The Wheel of Fortune

The Justice

The Hanged Man

Death

Temperance

The Devil

The Tower

The Star

The Moon

The Sun

Judgment

The World

The Fool

Chapter 5: The Minor Arcana..................................48

The Four Suits

Looking at the Numbers

Chapter 6: The Spreads That You Should Learn.....54

The Self-Identification Spread

The Aries Spread

The Taurus Spread

The Gemini Spread

The Cancer Spread

The Leo Spread

The Virgo Spread

The Libra Spread

The Scorpio Spread
The Sagittarius Spread
The Capricorn Spread
The Aquarius Spread
The Pisces spread

Chapter 7: More Tarot Spreads to Help You Get Started and Mix It Up..73

Self-Diagnosing a Disease
A Spread to Celebrate the New Year
The Pyramid Spread
A Spread to Help with the Week Ahead

Chapter 8: How to Move Beyond the Deck.............80

Using the Tarot Vocationally
The Options You Have for Your Business
General Tips to Help You Start with Your Tarot Readings

Chapter 9: Tips to Help with Your Tarot Readings..91

Find Your Tarot Card for the Year
Gather Together a Few Decks
Pull Out a Daily Card and Learn from It
Download an App About Tarot Cards
Make Some Charts for the Daily Pulls You Get
Learn What the Card Wants You to Know
Find a Study Buddy to Work with You

    Associate Your Own Chosen Keywords with Each of the Cards
    Start Out with the Court Cards First
    Try Doing the Readings with the Major Arcana Alone

Chapter 10: The Danger of Tarot – Things to Know About Misusing Tarot...104

    Taking Some Cautionary Measures
    Cleansing Your Deck
    The Real Danger of These Cards
    Stick with What You Know

Chapter 11: Tips for the Beginner of Tarot Cards...118

    Don't Try to Overreach in the Beginning
    Consider Keeping a Tarot Journal
    Always Remember Who Is in Charge
    Keep It Simple
    Find a Way to Create a Personal Connection to the Cards
    Learn How to Reach Your Higher Self
    Swap Out for a Simple Spread
    Read the Picture That Is on Your Card
    Tune into What Your Intuition Is Telling You
    Perform Some Tarot Readings for Yourself
    Forget About the Rules for a Little Bit

Find Out What These Cards All Mean to You

Use the Tarot in a Mindful Manner

Conclusion..134

© Copyright 2018 by Judith Guise - All rights reserved.

The follow eBook is reproduced below with the goal of providing information that is as accurate and reliable as possible. Regardless, purchasing this eBook can be seen as consent to the fact that both the publisher and the author of this book are in no way experts on the topics discussed within and that any recommendations or suggestions that are made herein are for entertainment purposes only. Professionals should be consulted as needed prior to undertaking any of the action endorsed herein.

This declaration is deemed fair and valid by both the American Bar Association and the Committee of Publishers Association and is legally binding throughout the United States.

Furthermore, the transmission, duplication or reproduction of any of the following work including specific information will be considered an illegal act irrespective of if it is done electronically or in print. This extends to creating a secondary or tertiary copy of the work or a recorded copy and is only allowed with express written consent from the Publisher. All additional right reserved.

The information in the following pages is broadly considered to be a truthful and accurate account of facts and as such any inattention, use or misuse of the information in question by the reader will render any resulting actions solely under their purview. There are no scenarios in which the publisher or the original author of this work can be in any fashion deemed liable for any hardship or damages that may befall them after undertaking information described herein.

Additionally, the information in the following pages is intended only for informational purposes and should thus be thought of as universal. As befitting its nature, it is presented without assurance regarding its prolonged validity or interim quality. Trademarks that are mentioned are done without written consent and can in no way be considered an endorsement from the trademark holder.

Introduction

Congratulations on downloading *Tarot for Beginners*, and thank you for doing so!

The following chapters will discuss everything that you need to know in order to get started with your own tarot readings today. There is a lot of misconceptions out there about the tarot readings and how to do it—but this guidebook is going to spend some time looking at what these tarot cards are all about, as well as how you can become a practitioner and learn them in your own life.

To start out this guidebook, we are going to take a look at the history of the tarot card. The tarot cards may have started out as a simple parlor game—one that people would play in social situations—but as the world of the supernatural started to grow, these cards changed more into what they are today. From there, we are going to take a look at the art of tarot and a bit about how to read some of the tarot cards that you have.

From there, we are going to look at the Major Arcana and the Minor Arcana. Both of these are important parts of the readings—and when you combine them together, we are able to get the full tarot deck to complete the readings of our choice. We can then move on to a few chapters on the different types of spreads that you are able to do as a tarot reader. We will look at some of the readings that you can do specifically for the different zodiac signs, as well as some of the other types of spread that you may want to use.

To finish up this guidebook, we are going to look at some more of the different spreads you can learn, how to move beyond the deck to get more out of this, the tricks to really getting the best tarot readings that you can do all of the time, and some of the things that you need to be cautious about when you decide to use the tarot readings.

There is so much that we are able to learn about and love when it comes to using the tarot cards. It is as easy or as complicated as you would like to make it, and this guidebook will help you to take this a bit further and either learn for the first time or enhance your knowledge of how these cards can be used for divination. When you are ready to learn some more about the tarot cards, make sure to read this guidebook to help you out.

There are plenty of books on this subject on the market—thanks again for choosing this one! Every effort was made to ensure it is full of as much useful information as possible. Please enjoy!

Chapter 1: The History of the Tarot

Before we start to take a look at the different meanings of Tarot, it is important to have a little bit of the history of this kind of process and how it has changed throughout the years. Tarot is going to be a type of card game that is designed to tell fortunes and even reveal the future. However, even though this is the way that tarot cards are used now, that is not the way that it started out.

In the beginning, tarot was just a deck of cards that were used in order to play games with others socially. They were only going to have the original 56 cards in them, and they didn't really look like anything that we will see today. In the beginning, the deck for tarot was pretty simple. There was no Major Arcana section at all. Instead, there were just the court or face cards, as well as the remaining 40 suited cards, with each suit counting from ace to ten—and while we are talking about it, the early days of the tarot are actually a lot more recent than you may think, happening in the late 14th and early 15th centuries.

While there are many different forms of divination that ancient cultures and civilizations probably used, it is unlikely that the actual tarot deck of today existed anywhere across time except around the turn of the 15th century. There has been no archaeological proof of this longtime connection, and we really have no historical proof of the existence of the tarot until we get to Europe during this time.

Despite this kind of history, which places the first decks of the tarot being released and played (often in a casual kind of card game rather than a tool of divination) around 1375, it is possible that the ancient mysteries, as well as the archetypes that are revealed in the Major Arcana cards, which didn't come into the deck until 1450, were actually passed down from ancient cultures across the world.

The symbols of the tarot cards help to bring in some of the mystique that is found there, and they often seem older than time itself. This is why a lot of people are going to guess that the tarot was much older in history than it really is and may be part of why people throughout the world are able to relate to these cards. The symbols are able to speak to us in ways that are hard to put into words, and that is basically the essence that is seen with divination. Despite this, though, the images for both the Minor and the Major Arcana cards were not added to this deck until years later.

Let's take a look at the history of these tarot cards a bit more. To start, Tarot was a type of parlor game that was called Triumph, and it was played in a manner that is similar to how Bridge is played today. The game didn't have any intention of divination at the time. However, around the turn of the 17th century, the people of Europe started to really show an interest in divination more and more, and this was when people started to add a much deeper meaning to the cards that they were looking at.

During this time in history, the deck would have consisted of a detailed Major Arcana section, and then the Minor Arcana section would have been far simpler—and then we have the court or face cards that may have been beautiful, but then, we come back to the pip cards, which are the ones that are numbered from ace to 10 and would have been really simple with just the cups, coins, wands, and swards, and nothing else on them.

Even when we get as far as the turn of the 19th century, the deck was still something that was incredibly simple, without too much adornment on the pip cards. However, people during this time became even more fascinated in the tarot as a means of divination, and this was when we started to see some major changes to the cards and how they were used. This was the time period where the divination became more popular compared to the parlor game of the past.

In fact, it wasn't until 1791 when the first divination-only tarot deck was designed and then released in Europe by Jean-Baptiste Alliette. This French man was into developing the imagery on the Major Arcana and the court or face cards in an extensive manner. However, at this time, the pip cards were still neglected quite a bit. It wasn't until later on, when the turn of the 20th century occurred, that Arthur Waite teamed up with the artist Pamela Colman Smith to design the cards as we know them more today.

The Debate of the Origins

There are a lot of legends out there when it comes to the tarot cards. There are some legends out there that say that this deck originated in Ancient Egypt. There are also some popular theories out there in the late 18th century that help to support this claim, but there hasn't been a lot of historical information to help show the connection.

While the Egypt connection was one that a lot of people believed in and followed, there are also some legends that the tarot deck originated in the culture of the Gypsies. It is easy to see some of the mystical images on the card and then associate them with the eccentricity and the occultism that is known from the Gypsies throughout time—and since there are a lot of thoughts in popular culture that has kept with this kind of stereotype, it is not something that hasn't had a lot of theories along with it as well.

Another thought is that this tarot deck originated from the Kabbalistic Jewish practice. The reason for this is that the symbols on the Major Arcana match the same number as paths to follow in the Kabbalah's Tree of Life. There are going to be 22 of each, and the symbols are able to align up with this almost perfectly. While it is fun to speculate about this, there is not a lot of historical information to help back it out. It is more likely that the rise of the occultist interest around the turn of the 20th century in Europe influenced tarot deck artists to create decks that appeared as if more Kabbalistic secrets had been infused all along. However, it is likely that Egyptian symbolism, Hermetic Mysticism, and more crept into the decks as well.

The truth is that there may be a mixture of a lot of different things in the tarot cards. It is a mystical divination tool that has gained a lot of popularity—and since this started to grow and the artists had to work with a game of playing cards along the way, that each artist used their own imagination to make it happen. Over time, a few of these maybe started to combine, and it leads us to an almost mystical look on the cards.

However, in reality, the tarot cards came from Europe. There may have been some borrowing from a lot of different cultures over time to add in the mystic that is needed with these, but that is not meant to say that one of these groups or another were the ones solely responsible for the tarot cards at all.

Learning about the tarot card is so interesting and can help us understand more about all of this in no time. These cards were not designed in order to help us learn about divination at all. They were originally designed as a way to help us to play a game that is similar to our modern day bridge. However, because there was a growth in interest to divination over time, this deck started to evolve and change over time—and now, we have the tarot cards that we have all come to know and love!

Chapter 2: Learning the Art of Tarot

Now that we know a bit more about the history behind the tarot card, it is time to take a look at some of the art that comes with using and reading the tarot card. Regardless of how old this practice is, tarot is a divinatory art that is going to use connections to the collective unconscious, numbers, and symbols in order to express its meaning. It is designed like a card game that has 78 cards, rather than the standard deck that is only going to have 52 cards.

You will quickly find that working with the tarot is not going to be like playing a game with the standard deck of cards, either. Tarot is going to rely on ancient mysteries to help establish the visual truth—and by arranging out the cards in a certain manner and learning how to read the cards in the proper manner, you are able to receive some insights into your illness or issues. It is possible, if you do this in the proper manner, that you will obtain some messages from your higher self and the universe.

Connecting with your Intuition

Tarot card reading is going to be so much more about connecting to one's higher self than it is about divining the inherent truth of the cards. The cards are always going to contain the same images and the same basic meanings. But it is going to be your shuffling and intentional questioning of the deck, that the cards group into arrangements that will reveal some deep and lasting truths that are going to be able to resonate for the querent.

However, you need to remember here that the cards are not going to be entities of their own that hold power with the tarot. And the querent (or the person you are drawing the cards for our about) isn't either. The reader of the cards is going to be that entity, and their higher self is going to be the center of all that power to help read and use the cards properly.

When you decide that it is time to embrace tarot and start to read the cards, you have to remember this truth when it is time to proceed. It doesn't really matter which of the deck options that you choose. It is going to be more important how you decide to use the cards of any deck. Use the deck for growth and healing purposes, and you will never do any harm to anyone else.

You have certainly heard a lot of rumors out there that Tarot is evil, unholy, or that it is going to invite in spirits that are going to harm you or the other person you are reading for. Tarot is not about that kind of stuff at all. Tarot is simply a process about the read of the cards being able to connect with their own higher power—a higher power that we all already have, whether we recognize it or not—and then answering questions for the other person. If you are able to do that, then there is nothing evil or worrisome about working with the tarot cards.

When you decide to engage in reading the cards for yourself, remember the importance of your own intuition and then use that to direct the channel to your higher self. If you ever feel that something we are writing down here doesn't seem to line up with the intuition that you are getting, then don't try to force it on yourself. Your intuition is going to be the highest truth possible, and it is much more valuable and powerful than anything that I can write down on the page.

Choosing Your Deck

Choosing the deck that you are going to use for tarot can either be a fun and exciting time, or it can be a stressful time when you are learning how to read tarot. There are a number of different decks that you are able to choose from. If you are searching online, it is possible that there are hundreds or more options available from all corners of the world. There are a few things that you are able to keep in mind when it is time to pick out the tarot cards that you want.

First, remember that intuition. Your intuition is going to be your own inherent connection with your higher self. As you try to pick out the tarot deck for yourself, it is important to use this as a chance to let your intuition as your guide. So, gather a few tarot decks that you really like and then hold them in your hand. Sit with these options for a bit and try to turn off your thinking mind. If you can, enter into a new state of meditation and see which one stands out to you and best suits your needs.

The Different Types of Deck

It is sometimes hard to pick out a deck because there are so many different types. In order to make it easier, it is helpful for you to know that some decks are going to be specifically for tarot readings, and then there are those that are known as Oracle Decks. These are going to be completely different.

With a tarot deck, you are going to have 78 cards that are divided between 22 Major Arcana and 56 Minor Arcana. The Oracle decks are going to be a bit different, though, because they can have as many or as few cards, as you would like, and each one is going to have its own Major Arcana card with lots of meanings and themes. And these Oracle decks are not going to include any court or face cards and no numbered pip cards. If you would really like to work with the tarot readings, it is best to avoid the Oracle decks.

Another tip is that some of the decks of tarot that you want to work with may be more oriented towards a theme that sticks out for you. There are different options like gay culture, Egyptian themed, black cat, Animal Wisdom, and so on. The second that you type in the term tarot deck online, you will start to see the big difference in the options that are available for you.

There are also decks that are going to have cards that are large and those that have the cards be small. Most people find that they like to work with bigger cards because they are easier to read—if you go with a deck that has some sort of explanatory book to go with them to help you out and ensure that you know what is going on.

Generally, there are a few pros and cons that you want to work with in order to make sure that you are going to find the deck that is going to work the best for you. Some of the benefits that you want to look for in the tarot deck you decide to go with includes:

1. Large card size
2. A theme that is relatable and that you are drawn to
3. A theme that is not easily seen
4. A package that has a detailed book that can help you out

5. A deck that is for tarot, rather than one that is considered an Oracle deck
6. Relatable art that you like

    a. Make sure that you are comfortable with the art that is on the cards. There are some decks, for example, that only show people who are white. Some practitioners are not going to care about this, and others are going to be bothered by this, so check out the deck ahead of time.

7. It feels like the deck chose you and is the most natural choice for you to go with.
8. A good paper quality
9. A good review of the product if you choose to go with an online purchase
10. The thickness of the card is good enough that you will be able to use it for a long time.
11. It is affordable within your means. The tarot cards, like almost any product, are going to come in at a lot of different prices based on how much you are willing to spend.

Then, there are the cons that you need to watch out for. If you see more than one of these things with your deck that you are interested in, then it is probably not the best option for you to purchase. Some of the cons that you need to be careful about when it comes to picking out the tarot cards that are the best for you include:

1. The cards are too small that you are not able to read them well.
2. They are not in a theme that you like at all.
3. You feel that the theme of the cards is too loud and that it distracts from what you are trying to do with the readings.
4. There isn't a book that comes with the package.
5. You do not like it, or it doesn't work for your needs.
6. You are looking at a deck that seems to be an Oracle deck, rather than a tarot deck.
7. Poor quality of the card, which makes it hard and fragile to work with.
8. You feel like someone else actually picked out the deck for you rather than being able to choose the deck.
9. The review for a particular online purchase is pretty low for the product.

Picking out the right deck to help you get started with your tarot reading is going to make a big difference in how well you are going to be able to do with the tarot reading. Take your time picking out the deck that you would like to use, and really pick the one that is best for your needs. Once you find the perfect deck, it is going to feel right—and learning how to read the deck is going to be so much easier overall.

Chapter 3: How to Read the Tarot Cards

Once you have chosen the deck that you would like to work with, it is time to explore a bit more about how you can read these tarot cards. Tarot is going to be a great divination art that will help you to better connect with the realms that are deep inside and outside the self. It is a great tool to use in order to provide flourishing support balance and growth to anyone's life.

There are a lot of different things that you are able to do when you use a tarot deck. It might all look the same if you are just randomly shuffling and drawing out the cards. However, if you put some intention behind the use of the cards, it is going to change things up and can really increase the potential benefits that you get with this one. Let's take a look at some of the different ways that you are able to use the tarot cards to help you make some of the best decisions possible with your readings.

Decision-Making

Tarot is a great tool to use if you would like to be able to boost up your own decision-making abilities. So many people feel unsure or indecisive about some of the big decisions that occur in your life. They may even hope for some growth, but they are not able to figure out which direction they should take. Tarot is great because it is going to provide you with decision, resolution, growth, direction, and so much more just through the deck.

With the assistance of the tarot cards, there are a few benefits that you are going to be able to get when it comes to decision making. Some of the things that you are going to be able to do with the assistance of the tarot cards includes:

1. Assert your values and your ideal situations
2. Assess the outcomes that are the most likely
3. Discern your motivation
4. Make some of the easier decisions you have with just a few pulls.
5. Uncover some of the reasons that you have a disease or illness along with your fears and anxieties.
6. Learn the best way to own up to the mistakes that you have.
7. Choose the right life path for you with lots of confidence.

Quality of Life

Tarot is able to remind you that you, and no one else, is in charge of your own life. Sometimes, it seems like we have no control over the life that we are living, and this can get really frustrating and tiring over time. But you are the one who gets to control the things that go on, and you just need to stand up and make it happen.

When you ask questions of the tarot, the answers that you are getting will come from your higher self, and they are often going to be transformed with some divine intention. These answers are never going to direct you to failure or floundering or a loss. They are there to help urge you to the growth that you want. With that in mind, though, you are the one who has to choose whether or not you follow the path that the cards reveal to you. Look forward to some of the benefits below to your life when you work with the tarot cards:

1. A better understanding of the amount of will power you have
2. An increased amount of trust in your own intuition and the higher self
3. Enhanced self-awareness and consciousness of the world
4. An increased potential to be more creative and express yourself in a more creative manner
5. Developed, focused, and honed psychic abilities
6. An amplified ability to be able to empower not only yourself but those around you
7. More empathy and compassion for those around you

Insight and Life Help

Many times, the tarot cards are going to be able to provide you with some more insight into your circumstances and can assist anyone in need, whether they would need help with clarity, assistance, direction or something else. The tarot spreads are designed out for this task, and we will take a look at some of these in a little bit.

With the tarot cards, you are going to learn how to connect with your own intuition, higher self, and psychic abilities, and this is going to aid you in so many ways. In addition, both the readers and the querents are going to be able to experience an enhanced and increased ability to heal and receive guidance from the universe. Take the time to ask the cards two questions, one that is short or one that is long and detailed. No matter what with this, you are going to receive some helpful insights that will direct the way that you should go.

Helping Others Around You

As you learn more about the tarot and begin to master it a bit, you will find that it is easier to become more empathetic, knowledgeable, and willing to help out some of those around you. You will find that the capacity for patience inside of yourself is boosted and as a reader of the cards, you are more likely to carry that responsibility of being patient with others.

When you have this kind of knowledge, you are going to be able to carry around information about all of the archetypal energies that are known to humankind across time. You are going to carry these stories, bear the burdens, and even hold the key that will unchain all of our shackles. As you are able to grow more in your appreciation and knowledge of tarot, don't hesitate at any time to ask questions that are going to benefit individuals, whole groups, or the whole Earth as a planet. Don't let your scope be limited with this, and learn how to proceed the way that you need without any fear.

There are a lot of different things that you are able to learn about when it comes to the tarot cards. Learning how to read them, as well as when to use them, while also being able to trust yourself in the process, is really going to make a big difference when it is time to really get the full meaning that these cards have to offer to you.

Chapter 4: The Major Arcana

There are a lot of different cards that we are going to need to focus on, but for now, we are going to look at the Major Arcana cards, as well as how they can speak to us. We can then look at some of the common spreads, along with the face and court cards that will go with them.

The Major Arcana cards are going to be able to reveal to us the inner mysteries of humanity. They are going to tell us the full story of humanity in the form of 22 archetypal images, and each piece of this story is going to tell us some deep truths about the nature of existence as a human in this world. The 22 cards are going to be numbered from either 0 to 21 or 1 to 22.

To help us better understand how these work, let's divide up the 22 cards of the Major Arcana and learn more about what each one of them means and how you are meant to read them.

The Magician

This card is all about being able to see your path ahead and about taking actions and making decisions. This is a card that tells you to follow your dreams. It talks about how you have already taken the time to be introspective, but now, it is time to stop thinking and start taking action. This can represent a very powerful source of inspiration that is ready to act as your muse, and it can predict that it is time to work on some complex projects now. It can stand for finding your flow, embracing your power, activating your energy, taking the first steps, and being more active because power and success are in your future.

In reverse, this card can signify that maybe your flow is blocked for some reason. There may be a few projects that you dream about, but they just aren't working the way that you want. Sometimes, it may not be your fault. Looking at some of the cards that show up around this one will help you find more clues about what is causing this blockage.

The High Priestess

This card is important because it is going to discuss how you can appreciate the feminine that is throughout the world. You will find that this card suggests the value of depth, reflection, sensitivity passivity, contemplation, and stillness. This card will tell you that it is possible for your dreams as long as you are open to the mysterious feminine energy that is inside of you.

When we see this one, it is a good signal that we need to take a step back from things and start to access the divine feminine grace and insight around us. It is a good signal that it is time to tone down your energy a bit or to remember that you are caught up in some delusions that are distracting you too much. It is time to find stillness and refocus so that things don't go too far and turn into a disaster.

The Empress

This card is going to suggest that there is something of abundance that is coming your way. This card is going to show the potential of abundance through different manners such as through reproduction and through financial prosperity depending on how it is used and what is asked. For those who are looking at it in the way of reproduction, this card signifies creation and fertility. If you are looking at it in other terms, it is going to represent that there are some fertile ideas found inside of you and you have a lot of potential in order to start using them to see financial growth.

When you look at this one upside down, this is going to have the opposite effect. It could represent some things like repressed truth, poverty infertility, and impotence. With these in place, you may find that it is hard to achieve the abundance of the Empress. Look at the surrounding cards here to get some more clues on how to get rid of the blockages and to improve your life.

The Emperor

Another card to look at is the Emperor. This one is going to represent the quintessential divine masculine. This one is all about the successful accomplishments, order, protection, leadership, fatherhood, and power. When you pull out this card, it suggests in many cases that success is imminent. As long as you are able to use the strength of the will and your clear, focused intellect, you are able to achieve anything that you set your mind to.

This card is going to represent a father figure or another paternal entity in your life that you could be getting along with, or one that there is some struggle with. In reverse, the Emperor is going to show what is going to happen when the authority is lost. This could be an unproductive revolution or even tyranny. This reversal sometimes shows us that there is a lack of focus or even a loss of a father figure in your life.

The Hierophant

This is a card that is going to represent the importance of learning, routine, and tradition. This one can often show up in a reading to help you to take counsel of those you trust the most before you make any big decisions in your life. It is also going to serve as a reminder that you should value those people whose counsel you trust the most.

This card is going to encourage the follower to stick with established traditions, while also accepting that there are some limitations in the tradition that some can't withstand. For these individuals, this card is going to represent what is standing in your way to reach the success that you want. For those who like and embrace tradition, this card is going to represent the beginning of the journey that you will take to self-actualization.

When this card is reversed, it is going to signify what happens when tradition is thrown out, usually the free flow of wisdom, lots of rebellion, and chaos. While this may seem like a great situation for some, there are a lot of people who are going to find this worrisome—when this card shows up, watch out for some kind of rejection or a shift in values.

The Lovers

This card is going to represent the love that is coming your way. In some cases, though, it is going to insist that you are not going to be able to handle the love if you are not able to find a way to appreciate and love yourself. This card is going to be a signal that your twin flame is headed into your life, but it also is going to represent that you have a very urgent need to start falling in love with yourself, and not always putting others in front of you all of the time.

When this card is reversed, it is going to signify that struggles in love are ahead of you. This is going to include a lot of different emotions like chaotic love, separation, indecision, and jealousy, to name a few. If you are going through and get this card, but you don't have a partner right now, it could show that there are some issues that are showing up in your own personality that are keeping you from experiencing this kind of love. If you want to know how to fix this issue, look at some of the cards near it to give you clues.

The Chariot

This is the card that is going to signify that any issues that are currently in your life are going to be resolved soon. It suggests that by embracing some of the control of your life is going to allow you to find both the peace and the change that you want in the situation. This card is going to insist that there is development, understanding, journeying, triumph, success, mastery, and growth, but none of this is going to happen without first struggling through conflict. That means that this card is going to assume that you have either gone through a trial recently or are dealing with it right now, and it will be resolved soon.

This card is important because it is going to show how even someone who is successful is a work in progress. When we look at the reverse Chariot, it means that there was some interruption in your path to success or that there are some big failures that are going to stand in your way. It can also see that you have an upcoming danger that will affect your personality, or it can show a lack of control in your life that is going to lead to burnout.

Strength

This card is going to demonstrate the peace of the Goddess that is shown within each person. Both women and men have this goddess blessing in them, one that expresses itself as compassion, charisma, understanding, and patience. This card is going to signal that the reader is able to see our blessings and that these are being used to our advantage. Strength is also going to signify the importance of courage and faith in all of us and helps us to remember to get back in touch with some of the inner wildness in order to honor our highest selves.

When this card is in reverse, it is going to signify that there is a lack of courage that is going to border on fear. Instead of working with our own blessings and being brave, the reverse of this card shows that many of us are dealing with hopelessness and torment. If you see this one, look out for places in your life where weakness or indecision could be holding you back and try to find some stillness to add into your life as well.

The Hermit

This card is an indicator that there is an intense transformation that is going to meet you soon, but it also suggests that you need to spend some time alone in order to embrace this kind of path. This card is going to force you to face these elements that are holding you back from the transformation, and it will remind you that there is a big connection between you and your higher self. When you have been able to access some of the alone time, this connection is going to be developed and strengthened so much more.

If you get the reverse of this card, it is time to take a look at some of your social patterns to see if you have isolated yourself so much that it is too hard to keep on growing. Sometimes, this is a healthy amount of alone time, but then it turns into something that is toxic, such as when you are done with a betrayal, a crisis, or a breakup. To ensure that you remain productive, embrace this shadow time as something that is temporary, something that is then going to lead to the growth that you want.

The Wheel of Fortune

This card is meant to suggest that much abundance is going to come to your life. It shows that you are able to gain a lot of rewards out of your current situation if you just let things happen. If you receive this card in a reading, it means that one season of the self is about to end so that there is more room for a powerful season to come in. This one is often going to represent the wisdom of the Hermit put into action. It is the step that you need to take after the Hermit's isolation to get what you need out of life.

When this is reversed, it shows that you are being faced with some sort of change, but for some reason, you are ignoring it quite a bit. This card shows that the internal harvest that you went with was bittersweet, rather than as productive and good as you had wanted. And there may be some times that are more difficult to open you up for the growth. The trick of this is to allow yourself to have some freedom to let go of what isn't serving you any longer.

The Justice

This card is going to show that there is a clear path to success nearby. You will have access to clarity and balance to find that path. In addition, you will have to learn your own truth as intimately as possible. Those who pull this card out of the deck should know that an important dilemma is going to show up in your life at some point, and the choice that you make is going to really change the course of your life.

When you are working with this one, you need to make sure that you are actively choosing to respond to the dilemma rather than just reacting to the options that are there. Take the time to really think things out, and embrace what you think is truly the best option for you.

When this card is reversed, it is going to signify the existence of imbalance, dishonesty, and unfairness to others and to yourself. If you do get this card out of the deck, then take a look at your life and see if you are able to see where the imbalance is. Open a wide, discerning introspective eye toward yourself to figure out how this unfairness is controlling your life, even if you didn't mean for it to.

The Hanged Man

This is a card that is going to represent how your experience is going to become expanded, deepened, refocused, or intensified in the future. This figure is going to hang upside down on the card, and this is a positioning that is going to represent that there is a paradigm shift or a big change in your perspective. However, this shifting is nothing but positive. When this card shows up, it shows that there is a positive reversal that is about to come your way, so don't be scared when this happens.

If this card is going to show up in reverse, it signifies that there is going to be a big shift and a new paradigm, but you are having trouble adjusting to this at all. It could show that you are playing the victim, fighting some progress, or you have not reached the right level of self-awareness in order to handle this transition. Learn how to tune into your thoughts and even play a bit of devil's advocate with yourself to see if you can change this.

Death

This card is not as literal as you may think, so it is definitely not something to feel frustrated or scared about when you pull it out of the deck. Death is actually one of the most positive and inspiring cards in the deck if you read it the right way. Death does not mean that you are going to diet. It is going to signify that there is a full-on transformation in your life. One needs to submerge into the depths of the self before they are able to rise up with new power. Be prepared for a lot of passion, shedding, and intensity as you change over to a brand new transformation when you see this card.

When this card is reversed, it is going to be a signal that you are about to great the shadow side, but sometimes the outcome of all of this won't turn out as beneficial as you may hope—unless you go through and change a few things. This card in reverse will show that you will meet that shadow with fear, which is going to lead to a lot of pessimism, stagnation, and more.

Temperance

This card is going to signify that there is a potential for pain, lasting peace, magic, transmuted into something that is positive. This is a hopeful card to draw, and it often means that you have just finished with a period of great upheaval. Or it could mean that your knowledge about yourself in a spiritual sense has changed quite a bit as well. What you decide to do with this new knowledge is what is often seen as similar to what is done in magic.

When this card is reversed, it is going to signify that you are in a state of imbalance. You have lost your path and have been really argumentative with those who are around you. You may find that there is a feeling of being torn or fragmented in different directions, and it is time to bring all of these parts back together to help you reach your harmony again.

The Devil

This is another one that is similar to the death card in that it is not as terrifying as it seems. While it isn't going to mean that you are doomed or possessed, it can mean that someone or something is controlling you rather than letting you be the one in control. Consider how you let others make decisions for you or if you are obsessed about something on a regular basis. Maybe the loss of control is going to come from a potential addiction like stealing, drugs, cigarettes, and alcohol. This card is going to point out how you have been shackled and why it is so important for you to regain that will.

When this card is reversed, it is going to signify what you likely feared from the start. It could mean that there is a lot of unhappiness, abuse of power, lack of self-control to temptation, and some of the inner demons in you are coming back out. If you do get the reverse of the Devil card, be cautious about the way that you proceed from now on.

The Tower

This card is going to suggest that you remained imprisoned by that Devil card above and you had to find a way to fight your way out. Traditionally, this card is going to represent utter despair, devastation, destruction, conflict, and strife.

However, there is more to the Tower card, and it can end up being a bit more. If you draw this card, it means that you have decided to fight for something that you believe in, and you are trying to destroy all of the toxicity around you in order to succeed with this fight. The destruction that is found will come from your liberation.

The Tower in reverse is going to show that the concept of illumination, when you saw it, could have been daunting or frightening to you. It suggests that you have gone and shut yourself up in a tower rather than trying to break free from it. It could be along the lines of imprisonment and avoidance of responsibility when you pull this card.

The Star

This card is going to represent a beautiful and transcendent openness that will result when you have true illumination. This means that there was a happy resolution to all of the events that were signified by the Tower card. It also contains the potential for healing, wholeness, and completion of any detrimental cycles. If you draw this particular card, you can be proud while also being hopeful and calm because there are a lot of good things that are coming your way.

When this is reversed, it signifies what can happen when the Tower in reverse advances in time, including waste of time, stagnation, a loss of self-respect, and more. If you end up shutting yourself down to any of the illuminations that may come your way, it is not that surprising that you will need to shut yourself down to growth and progress as well.

The Moon

This card is going to take us a bit further than what we are going to see with the Star card. This is going to assert that the querent is a fully functioning psychic in training. If you do draw out this card form the deck, it is important to embrace the divine feminine in your life and learn how to stay true to the truth. Do not be afraid to greet your shadow self. You may need to be away from society for a bit of time, but this doesn't mean that you are isolated. You are on a spiritual journey for this time. Always keep an eye on the dreams that you have and remember that your imagination is able to do some incredible things.

In reverse, this card is going to signify that you are in a state of confusion that is brought about because you are not able to integrate your newfound faith and spirituality. If you do draw out this card, it is likely that you feel uncomfortable with the concept or action of the imagination. It is possible that you have been relying too much on substances to reach that spiritual growth.

The Sun

This card is going to represent everything that the sun usually symbolizes—including expansiveness, success, joy, happiness, and freedom, to name a few. This card suggests that you have started on your path to enlightenment and that you are currently feeling the clarity and focus in order to achieve all of your dreams, as long as you are able to stay with this path. You should be optimistic and not be afraid to share this knowledge with those around you.

If you get this card in reverse, the Sun is going to signify that the inner light inside of you has dimmed. You may see this if you aren't able to see things very clearly or you refuse to share your knowledge with others. Maybe you are arrogant and assume that you don't need to take the time to learn more. No matter what the situation is, this card reversed means that you doubt yourself.

Judgment

This card is another one that you are going to see with rebirth. It is going to insist that there is a new path to follow when you have settled into the energy that comes with the Sun card. The idea with this one is that when one door closes, there are a ton more that are going to open. It is also going to show us that the time to make a decision is now. There are going to be some changes ahead, and you are going to be tested to see if you are able to carry the light that you have right now.

The Judgment card in reverse means that you have heard the call to change and to act and to become reborn, but you have been ignoring it so far. You may not be really ready to understand what is at hand, but it could be because you are willfully choosing not to do anything. If you do end up pulling this card, consider how you may be acting out of a fear of change in your life.

The World

The World card is going to be another of the cards that will symbolize completion. Those who draw with this card have gone through a period where they have gotten a lot of success, and this brings them pride and satisfaction. This card is all about celebrating your accomplishments and dancing when you are done. It is about the union of the world with the self and about festivities that are all going to occur when you are in your prime. If you haven't currently achieved abundance, then it is right around the corner and will be yours in no time.

When this card is reversed, it is going to signify that there will be a delay in the success that you get. There could be some limitations that come into play, or you may feel like you are anything but free and validated. This is a sign that you are not quite done with the most important work. If you do pull out this card, it is best to wait out the situation you are dealing with—and soon, progress and movement will happen again.

The Fool

This card is going to open and close the Major Arcana, and that is because it is going to associate back with innocence, openness, and any new beginning. This is the idea of conception and closure, and it is a card of balanced extremes and energy that is focused through playfulness. If you draw this one, it could be because you are acting like a fool, but it could also mean that it is time to take a route that is less serious in order to succeed. Learn how to take yourself a bit less seriously and play around a bit more.

When the Fool card is in reverse, it means that you are playing out some of the qualities that are bad with this card. You are playful and childish, but you have taken this to the extreme and become foolhardy and irrational and naïve. Don't be afraid of change and of becoming more mature in the process as well. There needs to be a balance between being trapped in seriousness and routine all of the time, and of playing around and never progressing either.

These are the 22 cards of the Major Arcana, the ones that you will focus most of your time and energy on within the reading that you are doing. The Minor Arcana cards are going to be important as well, but it is going to help to enhance some of the other cards that you are pulling out in the beginning.

Chapter 5: The Minor Arcana

We have spent some time looking at the Major Arcana cards—now, it is time to look at the supporting Minor Arcana cards and how they are going to be able to work together to help get the full reading that you need. While the Major Arcana cards are going to be able to represent the long-term situations that you could experience, those that belong in the Minor Arcana cards are going to take a look at what is happening in your daily life. These will include the small struggles, thoughts, interactions, and even wins that you are going to face on a regular basis. They can even provide you with some insight into situations that happened in the past and will help to give you advice on the decisions that you need to make now in order to see an influence on your future.

The Four Suits

There are going to be four different types of suit cards that will make up the Minor Arcana. These include the Pentacles, Swords, Cups, and Wands. Each of these suits will contain 14 cards. These include 10 numbered cards and four cards that are known as the court cards. These court cards are going to include the King, Queen, Knight, and Page. Each of these four suits will represent a different area of your life so that you are able to know where to direct this guidance when one of these cards shows up in the Tarot reading. A quick meaning of what these suits mean includes:

1. The Wands: These are going to be all about action, invention energy, and initiative. They are going to help guide how you are able to move through your life and can give you advice on when to take action, and when it is time to hold back a bit.
2. The Cups: These are going to represent the relationships, intuition, and emotions in your life. These cards are good at guiding you in love and can help you to grow with the help of understanding the lows and highs of your feelings.
3. The Swords: These cards are going to bring up the challenges that come up in your life. They are going to give you a good idea of when any conflict and heartache are going to come about and can help you to harness the strength of your own mind.
4. The Pentacles: And finally, the Pentacles cards are going to be associated back with your finances and your work. These are the cards to look at when it comes to your health, family, money, and any long term goals that you have.

Looking at the Numbers

While the suits that we see with the Minor Arcana are going to show you which areas of your life need the most attention, exactly what energy is about to come your way will be shown by the number that shows up on the card. The numbers one through ten, along with the court cards, will carry with them a general kind of energy that can help you to really catch on to the message that you are getting when we get to the Minor Arcana. The meaning of the different numbers that you are going to see here includes:

1. Aces: Aces are going to represent a beginning. They will indicate the earliest stages of a new endeavor, potential, drive, and initiative.
2. Twos: These are going to carry a message about dichotomy and balance. When a two shows up in the reading, you are never going to be able to move forward until you are able to reach some kind of equilibrium.
3. Threes: Threes are going to be all about communication and your interactions. They are going to give a good indication to you about the influence that others are able to yield over your emotions, work, and life.
4. Fours: The "fours" cards are going to show us a break period that you are currently in. Before you are able to

move forward, you need to stop for a bit and then contemplate where you have been and where you would like to go.
5. Fives: The "fives" cards are going to be all about adversity. These cards are going to indicate that there is a conflict, a loss, or some other kind of negative experience that is going on in your life that you need to be able to overcome.
6. Sixes: This kind of card is going to represent some growth. It helps you to overcome challenges, leaving bad situations behind you, and being able to get the best understanding possible about who you are right now.
7. Sevens: These cards are going to be there to show you when it is time to have some faith in yourself and in the universe. There are a lot of things happening to you in your life right now, but with truth, determination, and confidence, you will be able to see it all through.
8. Eights: These cards are all about work and change. They are able to tell you that the only way to reach your goals and progress is to make some changes to what you are doing right here and now.
9. Nines: These cards are going to show us a bit about fruition. Things are starting to come together for you, and it is possible that you will either like or not like what you see right now.

10. Tens: These are all about the final outcomes and the end of a cycle that you are currently in. They are going to carry some messages about the consequences or rewards that you will experience for the work that you have put in.
11. Pages: This kind of card is going to represent messages and beginnings. The Pages will indicate that there is a new phase where you know what you want to accomplish, but you don't know how to do it. These cards are going to help you know that it is fine to gather up all of the information that you can before you take any more steps.
12. Knights These cards are going to be all about the movement. You know where you are going, and the Knights will tell you that it is now time to get those wheels in motion rather than waiting and messing around any longer.
13. The Queens: These cards are another one that asks us to take a look at our feminine message of power, advice, and cards. They may be there to tell you that it is time to ask for advice and help from someone who is wiser and has more experience.
14. Kings: The King is going to flex his muscles with power and authority. These cards tell you that you already have what it takes to succeed, but you must believe in everything that you are.

These Minor Arcana cards are important along with the Major ones, and when the two groups are put together, it is much easier to learn about where you should go in life, what has happened in the past, and what is likely to happen in the future. A Tarot reader will be able to put these all together in order to come up with a comprehensive outlook of the querent and what they should look for in the future.

Chapter 6: The Spreads That You Should Learn

Now that we have been able to go through and learn a bit about the different parts of the deck, you are now ready to do some of the things that are considered fun with the tarot reading and do some of the actual readings of the cards. This chapter is going to go through several different spreads that you may encounter so that you can have a bit of practice with the cards. Each of the spreads is going to come with a different intention or theme so that you know what to expect, even though the cards could surprise you and come out completely different.

However, before you do any tarot reading or any kind of spread, make sure that you do a cleanse of your deck. This is especially important if someone else has used or touched the deck for any reason recently. Then, shuffle through it well, and take some time to put yourself in the moment with all thoughts on what you would like to ask of the deck.

If you do need to cleanse the deck, this is a simple process, and the best technique to use when it needs to be done is to use smoke. A light stick of incense and running your cards through the smoke can help with this. Or you can apply the same technique with the smoke of burned sage bundles or other dried herbal bundles, resins, and incenses. You can also use crystals to help cleanse the deck. Pick out the method that you like the most, and then work from there.

Once the deck is ready, it is time to work with some of the different readings and spreads that you may encounter as you do your work. The first one is going to be a spread for the past, present, and future. For this reading, you are going to spend time focusing on three things; where you have come from or your past, where you are now, which is the present, and where you are about to go in the future.

Then, take your deck and only pull out three cards. So, cleanse the deck, shuffle it around, and then think about the elements of the past, present, and future. Think about what you have struggled through, and where you hope to be in the future. Lay the three cards that you pull out face-down first, and arrange them in any manner that you would like. However, make sure that the first card laid out is your past, the second is the present, and the third is your future.

Once you have them in the order that you would like, flip them over either all at once or one at a time to get your divine answers. You can look back through this guidebook to see what each of the cards mean and divine what is being said with each part.

Another spread that you can work out is one that will identify the three different aspects that are found with your Self. Just like with the last spread, you are going to pull out just three cards from the tarot deck. But the difference here is that you are going to think about yourself as a whole, rather than thinking about it as different moments of your life. After you have cleansed and shuffled the deck, you will choose to ask the cards to provide you with some glimpse at your life.

You can do this the way that works best for you. Maybe you want to ask about your three biggest weaknesses, your biggest lessons, job possibilities, or other aspects that are important about yourself. As with the first spread, you can choose to flip over all of the cards at once or go through and interpret them all one at a time.

The Self-Identification Spread

We can then move on to trying a spread that is about the self-identification. This one is going to take us a bit longer than the other options because there are going to be a few more cards that you need to pull out compared to the other ones. You will need to pull out ten tarot cards in order to complete this one, and they can be laid out in any manner that you would like. But the general idea to get this to work well for you is to turn the cards into the shape of a cross. If you would like some assistance with this one, there are some pictures online that you can use to help.

When you are shuffling the deck, make sure that you focus your attention on yourself or on your own personal life. Lay down your first card in the middle of the space that is in front of you. The first card is going to be there to represent yourself and your general relationship to whatever question you are asking about. Then, card 2 will be laid overtop the first card, but sideways to make a cross in that manner. This second card is going to represent any of the obstacles that are directly in the way of the path that you would like to take.

Then, there is card three that needs to be on the left of the first card. This card is going to be the one that represents what is behind you, what you have already been able to work through, and what knowledge or tools you are able to use as a result to your advantage. Card four will then go to the right of card one, and it is going to be there to represent what is generally ahead for you, and what you should spend some time watching out for.

Card five needs to end up right below card one. This is the card that is going to suggest something you have been able to grow out of or something that is beneath you and that you should learn how to evolve from if you haven't already. That leads us to card six, which is one that ends up above card one and it will talk about some of the best qualities that you possess, and the way that you will be able to access the higher self.

Now, when you take a look at the first six cards that are there, you should already have a nice cross shape that is there. Feel free to flip over these six cards at this time and then process what you believe they are telling you based on the question that you asked in the beginning.

But we still have four more cards that we need to focus on here. The four of them will go one after the other in a vertical line right next to the cross, over on the right side. Starting at the bottom, lay down card seven. This one is going to represent how you feel about moving forward with this new knowledge that you have. Then, lay down card eight above this one and see that it will demonstrate what the attitudes of the people around you will be in regards to this matter.

Right above the eighth card is going to be card nine. This one is going to talk about your greatest hopes and fears in terms of moving forward with the knowledge that you have gotten. And then we move on to card ten, which ends up above card nine, and it is going to suggest what should come next. When these are done, flip them over and then interpret the meaning of them alone, and then in reference to the original 6 cards that you had out.

This spread is going to take a bit more time to accomplish, but when it is all done, it is certain that you are going to have a lot of new answers about yourself figured out and ready with this kind of spread.

The Aries Spread

This is a spread that is going to work the best for those who are Aries. So, if you are not an Aries, but you are reading out these cards for someone who does have this sign, then it is a great option to work with. If you yourself are an Aries, then you can try to read this out for yourself to see what you are then able to discover about yourself as well.

For this kind of reading, you will need to come in and pull out seven cards. You can lay them out in any order that you would like, but the order is important here so remember which card you pulled out first, second third, and so on. In addition, it isn't necessary to ask a question with this spread because you can just learn from the cards as they fall, but you can add in a question if you feel that is better.

The first card on this spread is going to be a good representation of how you are doing physically while the second card is going to look at how high or low your overall energy levels are at this time. And card three is going to ask you how you are doing when it comes to the amount of control that you feel. This one is going to have something to say about whether you are uncontrolled or if you are focused on succeeding all of the time.

Then, we move to card four, which is going to talk about how excited you are for life and how much enthusiasm you are feeling on a regular basis. Card five is going to ask what you are trying to run away from, and card six is going to show you how to approach best any of those dreams and goals that you have. And then we get to the seventh card that is going to reveal the deepest and truest goals and dreams that you have. Lay down your cards one at a time and process them individually for the best results.

The Taurus Spread

Now, if you are not an Aries or you are doing a read for someone who is not an Aries, then it may be time to try out this one. It is similar to the one we did before, but it is going to be best if the reader or the querent is a Taurus instead. This one is going to be in need of seven cards, and you can lay them out in the order that works the best for you, as long as you are able to remember the order. You do not have to ask a question with this one if you don't want to, but if you have a question that is weighing on your heart or mind, then go ahead and ask about it.

The first card in this one is going to ask the Taurus to dig down deep and figure out what their own opinion or stance on money and possessions are at this very moment. Then, card two is going to take a closer look at the current state of your finances while card three will go a bit deeper by examining some of the skills and talents that you often use in order to make your income right now.

Then, we can move on to card four, which is going to give an estimate on whether the Taurus has been feeling any sexual pleasure recently (and if it says that there was a good sexual pleasure, it will discuss how the experience was), Card five is going to look at the way that the Taurus is able to relate to excess and luxury, and the sixth card is going to be taking a look at how patient the Taurus has been lately.

The final card in this one, the seventh card, is going to figure out the amount of jealousy and possessive the Taurus can be when it comes to things that are not considered a material good. Ideally, this kind of card is going to show where the biggest struggles for this person will be.

The Gemini Spread

This one is going to work for the Gemini reader or querent. It is going to work in a similar manner to what we saw with the other two, but it is going to pull out eight cards, and these are going to focus mainly on the issues that a Gemini is most likely to have to deal with as well so keep that in mind as you move along with this one.

For this one, we are going to look at card one and see how it talks about the way that your mind is working right now. The second card is going to check on the wonders and the truth and sees how well the person is able to lie about things at the moment. And then there is the third card that is going to wonder who or what you might be watching or researching right now.

The fourth card is going to talk about your family life and will check in with how things are going with you when it comes to your parents and siblings. The fifth card is going to take a look at communication and how that is working out for you right now. It will explore whether you fight more often than you agree with others. It will look at whether you communicate with others in an aggressive or a pleasant manner, and so much more.

We can then move to the sixth card. This one is going to discuss any of the doubts that the Gemini is going to deal with. It will ask what is holding you back with the power of doubt. And then there is the seventh card that wonders whether there are times when you are too dreamy or delusional. And the eighth card is going to be a kicker for the Gemini because it is going to look and see what your current relationship is with your inner twin, and what that inner twin is like.

The Cancer Spread

This is another one that is going to pull out eight cards to help you learn more about yourself and where you are going in your life. The first card with this spread is going to tell the person more about where they come from, including things like family circumstances, and some of the complexities that helped to shape them. The second card is going to ask about some of your current dreams, and card three is going to wonder how home life is right now.

Then, we can move on to the fourth card. This one is going to be more specific and ask how you view your father right now. Card five is going to take a look at how much you need a good security net to feel safe and happy in the world, and the sixth card is going to ask how, or how intensely, you are able to express your deepest feelings. Card seven is going to talk about your compassion and how kind and considerate you really are.

The deck is going to finish off with the eighth card for Cancer. This one is going to take a look at how psychic the individual is, or could be. It will also look at how advanced and awakened the abilities are right now and how you could work to improve them with some time.

The Leo Spread

This one is going to pull back and only need to work with seven cards to make the spread work. The first card is going to take a look at how intense or dominating the ego is for the Leo right now. Then, the second card is going to see the world as a stage and will look to see what part of that stage you are acting on right now. Card three is going to explore that inner child and see how healthy that child is. And we can then look at the fourth card to see how your love life is. This will look at how things are going romantically and how you are feeling about love and romance right now.

When we move on to the fifth card, it is going to examine how much compassion, respect and admiration you have four children and the sixth card is going to take a different view and see where you take risks in your life and where you really relish in the risky freedoms. And then the seventh card is going to take a look at the Leonine mane. While you may feel that you are the queen or king of the jungle, this one is going to take a look at whether you are a ruler who is generous or one who is wicked.

The Virgo Spread

This is a spread that is going to work well for the reader or querent, who is a Virgo, but it is going to rely on eight cards to tell us a bit more about ourselves. When you pull out the first card for someone who is a Virgo, it is going to let you know information about how you feel about your body as an aspect of yourself. Card two is going to reveal how much interest you are able to show when it comes to medical or healing studies. And card three will talk about the kind of physical health that you are enjoying at the moment and card four to ask how you are feeling about the work that you do.

Now, we can take a look at the fifth card, and this one will check to see if the analytical mind is working well, or if you are too critical of the people and situations around you. Card six is going to take a look at how well you are able to adjust when a hardship finds you, and card seven is going to reveal if you are a consistent person or someone who is more of a hypocrite in what you do. The seventh card can sometimes tell us if we are too much of a perfectionist.

And the final card, the eighth card is going to look to see if we have decided to distance ourselves from the life that we are in because we are too wary of what could happen if we let others get too close.

The Libra Spread

This is a spread that is going to take on a few more cards to help us learn more about the Libra. This spread is going to pull out nine cards to help us out. The first card that we are going to pull out here is going to be a look at decision making since many Libras have time making their decisions in a timely manner. Card two is then going to take a look at how well you are able to form a relationship or a social bond with those you meet.

The third card is going to help you get a good look at the way that you are able to bond with others in a vocational or professional setting, and then we can look at card four to see where in your life you need to strive for adding in a bit more peace to make life better.

Card five is a bit different because when we flip it over, we are going to be able to see the potential that we have for vengeance or forgiveness of others, and which of the two is the one that you move on to the most often. Card six is going to look closer at the intimate relationships in your life and will wonder what you give away to these lovers of yourself. Then, card seven is going to encourage the querent to see how they could be suppressing or repressing some of the feelings that they have.

When we take a look at card eight, it is going to help us see how artistic our feelings can be. And finally, we get to card nine. This one is going to take a look at what most Libras see as their own worst trait about how you act or appear to be sullen or phony.

The Scorpio Spread

This spread is going to be one that works the best for Scorpios and will need eight cards to make it happen and work the best. The first card when we are looking at the Scorpio spread is going to relate to the seventh card of the Libra spread above. It will look at what you are trying to suppress emotionally, and what seems to be the one that is suppressed the most out of all. Then, the second card is going to force you to face any of the taboos that are in your life while card three moves on to encourage you to embrace your own true sexuality.

Card four takes this a bit further and will show you how to conceptualize your own death, and card five is going to help you to look over some of the values that you hold as the most important, especially if you didn't know what those were to start with.

Card six in this spread is going to show you what legacies and birthrights are potentially going to be yours. And card seven is going to move us a bit over to be more personal because it is going to talk about some of your own tendencies for self-destruction if there are any there. And finally, we get to card eight. This one is going to equate you to water and will look at whether you are an ocean, a river, a lake, or a creek. Basically, this is going to look at how deep you are and what capacity you hold, for intellectual, emotional, and spiritual intensity in this life.

The Sagittarius Spread

This spread is going to be a bit smaller and will focus on just pulling out six cards. But it is going to make sure that we are able to take a look at some of the different things that are going to describe the person who is a Sagittarius.

In order to start, the first card is going to give us a good look at the way that we are interacting when we are in our social groups and will help us understand the role that we are playing in these social groups. Card two is going to examine the education level and the type of education that you have had up to this point, and the third card is going to look to your most firmly held beliefs or practices of religion at this time.

Card four is going to reveal to us the impact or extent of the adventuring and journeying you have done in the outside world while card five does the same for any traveling that you may have done, or that you are doing right now, in reference to the inner world that you have going on. And then we are on to the sixth card, which is going to show where you currently are on your life-long search for purpose and meaning, as well as what you are able to expect to meet you in the near future!

The Capricorn Spread

This is going to be a spread that asks you to pull out seven cards, exploring more about what is important to the Capricorn and how they are able to make the changes that are needed for their own lives. The first card with this one is going to help the Capricorn look at how you feel about the career that you are currently in and what hopes that you have for your future there. Card two is going to look at how intense your wishes for fame and power are. Some people have a higher wish for this, and some are perfectly happy where they are.

The third card of this is going to take a look at how you are as an individual. It is going to explore whether you are really intense for your wishes and dreams of power, whether or not you are responsible, and how serious you are about your goals. Then, the fourth card is going to show how the values that you hold dear are going to line up with the values that the rest of the world are going to hold.

The fifth card in the Capricorn spread is going to examine the relationship that you have held with your mother. And the sixth card is going to give you some key steps for aiming for the right goal and even talks about the right goals that you should reach to attain the success that you want. Finally, the seventh card is going to reveal what you are aiming toward all of this dedication, thoughtfulness, and hard work that the other cards have looked at.

The Aquarius Spread

This spread is going to pull out eight cards, and you can arrange them in any manner that you would like as long as you focus on them in the right order. The first card is going to tell you the closest friends in your life right now and what these people represent for you. Card two is going to show you your thoughts on freedom and if there are any aspects of your life that you are trapped with right now. The third card is going to point out your role in the group and let you know if you are a follower, a worker, a leader, or something else.

The fourth card is going to be all about the opposition in your life. This one is going to take a look at what you work against in the current society and what kinds of revolutionary urges, if any, you hold onto right now. Card five is a good look at the impulsive nature that is inside of you, and the sixth card is going to look at whether you feel worthy, inferior, or superior to those around you.

Card seven is the next option, and it is going to take a look at whether you are underestimating yourself or if your sense of self is going to be inflated. And card 8 is going to show you the path that you need to follow in order to live out your dreams and follow what the stars have in mind for you.

The Pisces spread

This spread is going to work the best for those who are Pisces, and the reader needs to pull out seven cards to make it happen. The first card is going to wonder at how optimistic and idealistic you are, or if you are more realistic and pessimistic instead. The second card is going to cut to the core of yourself and see whether you have a tendency for martyrdom and self-sacrifice towards those around you. And the third card is going to talk about the kind of spiritual path you are on and where it could possibly lead you.

The fourth card is going to help the Pisces know what they are addicted to in this life and the fifth card is going to reveal if there is any kind of hidden adversary that is coming into your life. The sixth card will point out if there are any metaphorical prisons that keep you stuck. And the seventh card is going to look at the path that is able to save you from these setbacks and that you get to look forward to when you are liberated from the previous prisons that you are in.

As you can see, there are a lot of different spreads to look at. The ones in this chapter focused mainly on the different zodiac signs, which can give you a lot of information and a great way to read the person who comes to speak with you about the cards. You simply need to ask them about their sign, and you are set to go!

Chapter 7: More Tarot Spreads to Help You Get Started and Mix It Up

In the previous chapter, we spent some time looking at some of the spreads that you can do based on the zodiac sign of yourself or the person you are doing a read on. These are great options to work with when you are trying to get started, and you want to make things unique for each person. However, there are so many other great spreads that you are able to do as well. This chapter is going to take a look at some of these spreads so that you can learn more about them and try out something more once you get those basic tarot readings down.

Self-Diagnosing a Disease

With this tarot reading, we are going to take a look at some of the other spreads that you can do, one that has nothing to do with the astrological themes we had before. Instead, we are going to use this one to help you to explain, to locate, and even decipher the source of any internal or external problem or disease that you have. To start out with this one, you will need to pull out 5 cards. If you can, it is best to sit down on the ground because you will want to arrange the cards like a star with you in the middle.

Once you are ready, you will take the first card and place it right in front of you. This one is going to signify the source of your power, the way that you gain energy, and the different ways that your body is going to use up that energy. Then, card two is going to be placed as the second point of the star to your right. This card is going to represent what you are feeling inside of yourself right now in terms of this disease. And the third card should go a bit behind you to the right. This one may suggest where that disease could come from, either emotionally or spiritually.

Then, we can move on to the left side with the fourth card. This one is going to be placed to the left and slightly behind you, and it is responsible for representing what influences of others or what struggles from your past could make the disease more of an issue right now. And the fifth card should be to your left to finish up the star. This card is going to signify how you are able to turn things around and how you can begin to approach self-directed healing for this kind of disease.

A Spread to Celebrate the New Year

This one is going to need a few more cards in it, 12 to be exact. But this is so that we can take a look at how each of the twelve months will turn out for you in the year. You will need to pull out one card for each month of the year. You can lay them all down face first before you turn them over one at a time to process. While you shuffle through this deck after you do the cleansing, you can either let the cards go through and generally predict the major themes of the year ahead or infuse the reading with a particular theme or question that you would like to have answered for you.

You can go through each month of the year and flip over the cards as you would like. Each card is going to give you an idea of what you are able to expect as you work through the year and can even help you to focus more on how you can make changes to improve your life in the coming year.

The Pyramid Spread

This is going to be a spread that is going to rely on six cards to get things started. The reason for this is that there are six different sides of the self, and each card is going to be laid out in a manner that will help you make a pyramid. Ancient Egyptians believed that there were many different facets that come with the self, some of which we are able to share with others freely, and some of which we are going to keep hidden. Because of this, there are going to be times when we will know the side we are told, but then there are going to be some sides during this reading that you may have trouble facing. But learning how to face it and accept it is going to help you to grow in ways that you never thought possible before.

When you pull out the first card, imagine that you are starting to work on what will be the base of your pyramid. You can leave it on its back and wait until you build up the entirety of the pyramid, or you can turn it over now and see the side of the self that you are proud of, the one that you have grown consciously and are eager to share with others.

Then, there is what we call the "second card." This one needs to end up to the right of the first card, and this is the side of our self that we are ashamed of and that we like to try and keep hidden from all others. Card three is going to be to the right of the second card, and it is going to suggest the side of yourself that you are able to sacrifice anything for others, also known as the martyr side.

Then, we can look at the fourth card, which is going to establish the second row of your pyramid, so put it above cards one and two and right in the middle of them. This is going to be the card that will demonstrate for us the side of ourselves that is a lover of knowledge and a type of scholar. For what area of study do you feel this kind of love the most, and what do you do in order to make it feel better. You can then put this in between card one and three, and this is the lover side of your personality. How do you love, who do you love, and how are you able to share this kind of love with the rest of the world?

Finally, we can move on to the sixth card. This one is going to be the top of your pyramid, coming in between cards four and five. This one is going to be the final aspect of your personal pyramid, and it is all about how you bring all of these facets together and fuse them so that you have your own self-expression and identity to work with.

A Spread to Help with the Week Ahead

This one is going to have a lot of similarities to what we saw with the New Year spread, which means that we have a card for every month of the year, the spread for the week ahead is going to require seven cards to cover all of the days of the week. Once you have been able to pull out these seven cards, arrange them out in the manner that you would like before turning them over.

When you are ready, you can turn them over, either doing one at a time to process them on an individual basis or doing it all at once. Whether you start the mental calendar that you would like to use either on a Sunday or on a Monday, the first card that you lay down is going to be different. Just go with what is going to work the best for you.

As you look at each of the cards and how they correspond with the different days of the week, go ahead and explore what each of these is going to mean for you. This gives you a good idea of what you are able to do during the week, what challenges are going to come up to you, and what you can do to ensure that you have the best week that is possible.

As you can see here, there are a lot of different options that you can work with in terms of the tarot card readings that you can choose to do. It all depends on how complex you would like to make it, how many cards you want to pull out, and even the questions that you are asking.

While it is true that some of these spreads of the tarot cards are going to be more involved and complicated compared to the others, they are all going to ensure that a beginner is able to get started with this and actually be able to read the cards and the messages that they offer. They are all going to be accessible, they are easy for anyone to understand, they provide a lot of insight, and they can help you learn more about yourself and others around you.

The neat thing about these is that they are just the beginning. They are meant to help you get a good idea of where to start. You can always add more parts to it and even make up some of your own over time if you would like. The tarot reading is highly personal and can be changed based on what you see with your own personal power.

Chapter 8: How to Move Beyond the Deck

If you are like a lot of people, just learning about the tarot and using it on yourself is not going to be enough. There is plenty to learn about yourself, but it is likely that after doing the readings as practice for a bit, you are going to want to take this a bit further and start doing readings on other people. This can really help to hone your skills more and can be really interesting to learn about the people around you.

This chapter is going to take a look at some of the things that you can do to move beyond the deck and start to work with others in their tarot readings. We will look at how to find the people who are interested, as well as some of the other things that you are able to do in order to see the best results with this.

Using the Tarot Vocationally

Using a metaphysical practice like the tarot is going to start you off on a lifelong vocation, but it is not always the easiest of tasks to work with. Turning the practice of tarot reading into a vocation, which can be a job that you do remotely, though a lot of those who like to work with tarot find that being up close and personal is a great way to earn a living with this and to really get to know the other person a bit more. This allows you a lot of options based on what you would like to do.

For example, you could start an app and have people visit there, or have your own shop where people are going to come and visit on occasion. You could also spread out with this gift through word of mouth, doing public work or private readings, and see where all of this is going to take you.

There are a number of steps that you are able to take the next step with the deck that you want to work within the tarot. Some of the questions that you need to ask yourself when you are ready to get started includes:

1. Where and with whom are you willing to work with? Also, consider where you are not willing to work and what kind of people you are not willing to work with.
2. What exactly are you planning to offer? Do you just want to stick with the tarot readings, or are you looking to expand to other things as well? Are you going to offer specific spreads or a wide variety? (It is fine if you want to expand out as you get better and learn more along the way.)
3. Do you plan on insisting on the clients meeting certain qualifications ahead of time?

4. What do you plan to offer that is going to be unique and different compared to what the competition is offering?
5. What do you plan to charge for your services? How will you decide to collect the payment? And are you going to have a sliding scale for the payment? Will the prices change as you establish yourself in the business?
6. How do you plan to promote yourself to others around you? Do you plan to work with some social media to promote yourself and talk to others? And if you do, which sites would you go with?
7. Can you program, or do you know someone who is able to program? If so, would you like to start your own app to ensure that more people are able to see your work?
8. Are you going to set up a website that will talk about your business a bit more and will help you to reach more customers?

These questions are good ones to go with to help you get your own business started and will ensure that you are set and ready to meet with the clients that you need for your business.

The Options You Have for Your Business

With the questions in mind above and they are answered, it is time to take a look at some of the different business options that you are able to work with. There are a lot of options here, depending on whether you would like to do this full time or part time and how much effort you would like to put into the whole thing. Some of the different options that are available for those who are first getting started in tarot readings for profits and who would like to find some clients to work with will include:

1. If you are brand new to doing the tarot readings, maybe meet up in a public space and do some weekly tarot readings. You need to make sure that it is fine for the business, but going with a diner, café, a library, and a park can work.
2. Find someone who owns a local business, and then offer to host tarot nights as a special offering.
3. Create your own app that you can promote and use to share some of your knowledge about the tarot readings.
4. Create a YouTube channel and podcast that you can use to reach your customers and share your knowledge.

5. Make the storefront for this kind of business is some social media page that is easier for others to find.
6. You may want to work with a blog about your knowledge about the tarot. It takes a few months to get it up and running and to ensure that others are able to find you. But it is a good way to get some of that energy out there. You can write out tarot inspired articles for your local newspapers and magazines as well.
7. You can buy your own literal storefront that you will have for just doing tarot and psychic readings if you would like to look like a more legitimate and professional kind of business.
8. Offer to do some of these sessions through the phone or on Skype and leave some fliers around your town with your number and some information about what you are going to offer.

As you can see, there are a lot of different options that you are able to work with when it comes to starting your own tarot readings. Thinking out of the box will make a big difference in how much you are able to do with this kind of business, and will ensure that you are able to find the right kind of clients to help you do more of these tarot readings.

General Tips to Help You Start with Your Tarot Readings

For those who are ready to work more with the tarot and are looking to take this to the next level, the steps that we are going to talk about in this section are going to provide us with some of the ideological and logistical backbone you need in order to start building up your own tarot empire for yourself and for others.

First, you need to start out small, especially if you are just learning how to work with tarots, and if you have not been able to build up your confidence in working with others. Keep the expectations about how this business will do realistic so that you can start to be surprised when things start to do well. You are welcome to start working on some of the ideas of how the business will do in the future, but don't worry too much about the details when you are in this phase of the journey.

When you start small, you give yourself more time to learn the trade and focus on what is going to happen in the future. You can spend this time exploring your options, meeting some of the great people who may become your clients in the future, becoming more confident in your readings, and remembering the passion that brought you to doing tarot readings in the first place.

The second step that you can do is to start out local. A great way to break into the local scene is to start out local and work with some of the business owners there whose ethics and vibes align with the energies of the tarot. You can maybe find an eatery or someplace else that is going to line up with the ideas of the tarot and use it to work your business. You may find some of the first clients you work with.

You should also look at finding a mentor to help you out. You never know who may be out there who would be willing to support you. This means that you should not be afraid to reach out to some of the potential patrons or others around the area to find a mentor.

A good place to start with this one is to find a good local business owner. These are great to socialize with about your love of divination. Even if they are not able to personally help you, they may be able to point you in the right direction to someone who is going to help you learn more about the tarot readings or about how to create your own business.

For example, imagine that you have been spending a lot of time at the local metaphysical store. You can chat with the owner each time that you come to the store, and you may notice that the owner is going to appreciate your hard work, the passion that you have, and some of the expertise that you are working on. You can then talk to them a bit more, and maybe you find out that this business owner is devoted to the tarot readings like you are. This could be a great opening to having some weekly lessons with them that will grow your own talents and helps you to gain more expertise.

There are a lot of people who can potentially become your mentor when you are working with your skills in tarot reading. It may take some time and some talent to work on, but over time, you are going to get better at this and will see the results and get some great advice along the way.

Next on the list to focus on is having some pride in what you are doing here. One of the most important steps that you need to focus on before you are starting up your own future tarot card reading business is that you need to maintain a lot of confidence and pride in yourself, your abilities as a psychic, and the knowledge that you have in the tarot cards. Even if you are brand new and have just started out with your readings, you need to have this kind of pride present, or no one is going to trust you to do the readings.

If you struggle with any part of it, fake it a bit and just keep practicing. Practice until you are able to remember the meanings of all the cards and then know that it is time to take some of these skills out to the world so that you can wow those around you. When you see that people are responding in a positive manner, use that good energy to boost up the amount of pride that you have in yourself.

During this time, especially when you are trying to build up your own business, take pride in yourself, and never feel bad or place some doubt in the skills that you have. It doesn't really matter in this step how people respond to you. You just need to have the right amount of confidence, remember why you love working with tarot in the first place, and then work with you. You are following your purpose (if this is truly a passion of yours), and that insists that you follow the path that is ahead with some pride.

Moving on up is the next step that you can focus on with all of this. Once you have had some time to work through the first four steps of this process, it is time to change up the scope that you are doing. As you work with your business and increase your knowledge and client base with the tarot card readings, you are really making some connections with those around you.

From here, it is time to work on a social media page or some other place where you are going to let your clients leave reviews about you. If you are able to afford it at this point, it is time to promote the page so that anyone who is nearby and interested in these readings is able to find your business and pick you out of the crowd. If you keep working with just a handful of clients that is great, but it isn't going to help your business to grow at all and can really slow you down if you want to turn this into a business that you love.

Promotion, good reviews, some advertisement, and some excellent readings will help you to grow your business bit by bit. And if you work steadily at this, you will find that it doesn't take long before you have a business that you can be proud of, while doing the work that you love.

Keep in mind during this stage that it is also important to ask your customers to provide you with some critiques and some honest reviews about your work. This allows you to know what you should work on over time and is only going to make you better. While it would be nice if you only got glowing and positive reviews all of the time, this is not really going to help you to improve your readings and won't get you ahead as you wish. As long as you are able to maintain your touch with your higher self, you are going to see success, even if there is some room for improvement.

Some people are just interested in learning about these tarot cards and what they are able to do with them. And that is fine. It is fun to be able to do some of your own readings and maybe impress your friends and family members with a few readings of their own. If this is what you decide to do with your own knowledge of the tarot cards, then that is just fine.

However, it is also possible to take your love and your passion for the tarot readings and turn it into a career. Whether you decide to do this on the side or as a full-time income, there are a lot of opportunities that come with this. There may be some hardships that tend to show up on occasion, and it may not always be as easy as you may have hoped in the beginning. But if you are willing to stick with it, and you are able to follow some of the guidelines that are above and in this chapter, you are going to love how you can turn this into a full-time income doing something that you truly love.

Chapter 9: Tips to Help with Your Tarot Readings

When it comes to working on these tarot readings, it is important for you to really work on how to boost your brain power and to connect with the higher power that is inside of each of us. This can be hard for some of us who don't realize all of the psychic abilities that are found in all of us. This is why we are going to spend some time with this chapter to learn more about the different brain boosters and exercises that you are able to do to help you see the most with the tarot readings that you are doing.

Find Your Tarot Card for the Year

With this exercise, you will need to learn more about the meaning of one card each year. The card that you end up choosing is going to be linked up with you, and it is going to become a big symbol for you over the following 12 months. When it is about time to celebrate the New Year, as the year number ticks up to one more, you will need to figure out your tarot Growth Card for the year.

All that you need to do for this one is to add the day and the month of your birthday with the digits of the new year. So, let's say that your birthday is 5/25/1961 and it is just about to turn to the year 2019. You would add 5 + 2 + 5. This is going to get you the answer of 12. Then, you would add 12 + 2 + 0 + 1 + 9 to get a number of 24.

With this, you would need to associate the number with its corresponding card in the Major Arcana. But then you look at this and see that the number 24 is going to be higher than the 22 cards in the Major Arcana. This means that you will need to add up the individual digits of the number to figure out the one that links with you. So in this example, you would add two plus four and get six. Your card, in this example, for the year is going to be the Lovers in the Major Arcana.

When you spend some time looking at this card closely to figure out the symbolism that is inside, and you analyze all of the potential meanings that come with it, you are going to be able to figure out what is going to come around for you in the new year.

Gather Together a Few Decks

This is an exercise that is going to make it easier to learn the symbolism that is in each card rather than just learning the words, meanings, and information that are packed inside of them. We can spend all day explaining what the cards mean, but sometimes it isn't going to stick with the person. This exercise allows you to get a bit more visual with your deck, which helps you to really learn about it more. And if you are able to work with more than one deck and combine them, you will be able to compare what the different artists were thinking about with each card, and you can learn so much more about it.

This type of close looking into the cards is going to be the best way to learn all of the messages that come with the images on the cards. There are so many different symbols and images found on each card, and closely looking at them is the best way to understand the meaning. It is far more useful than just reading any book on the subject.

Basically, with this exercise, if you are able to gather up a few different decks, from different artists, and you look through the imagery that is on the pictures, you will learn so much more about the meaning that is behind them. It also will help you to expand out your own appreciation of the cards greatly.

Pull Out a Daily Card and Learn from It

To help you learn more about your deck and become more comfortable with it over time, it is a good idea to start working with a pull of a daily card. This practice is going to be really helpful when we talk about newcomers to the world of tarot because it helps them to have a better understanding of their decks, and they will learn more about what tarot has to offer to them.

It is up to you what time of the day you would like to use to pull the card. But the point is that you draw a card each day to allow you time to practice while also boosting your psychic and divination abilities. For those who are brand new to tarot, this is a good exercise to work with, especially if you start out with all of the cards facing in the same direction.

Remember as we went through we spent some time talking about the reversed card option. This can work with some of the readings, but as you are learning your deck, just keep them all facing the same way. After a few months of doing this option, you can add in the reversed and start learning about that as well.

Download an App About Tarot Cards

If you don't already have your own deck, or if you are not interested in carrying the deck that you chose around with you all of the time, try downloading the app for tarot onto your tablet or phone. There are a lot of options out there when it comes to an app that works with tarot, and many of these are going to be free.

Many times, you are going to be able to find a lot of different features that come with the apps that you choose. Some are going to offer you options to help with daily readings and practice, bigger spreads of the tarot cards, individual card information, and sometimes it will provide you with a place to the journal based on what cards you decide to bowl.

Some people do not like to bring out the tarot app and would rather work with the cards that they have available. They may feel that this is not the same kind of thing and that they need to actually hold the cards in their hands to get the results. But the same rules can apply here as we talked about earlier. You are the one in charge, not the cards, and not the app. You can use anything that you would like in order to help you learn more about this.

Your higher self is the part that is going to guide the readings and who will help you to deliver the overall meaning of what you see. It doesn't matter if you are using the app or the actual cards. So, at least give one of these apps a chance. If you find that you like the cards because of the feel or you are able to connect with them better than the app, that is fine. But for some people working with the app can be the secret to making sure you are able to learn more about the cards, practice, and even learn some new spreads.

Make Some Charts for the Daily Pulls You Get

Sometimes, there are those who are going to connect better to the tarot cards and will have a better chance with them when they get to put in a little bit of work. And if you are one of those people who are extra studious and who love to make a lot of lists, then this is the exercise for you. That is because this exercise has the goal of allowing you to track the cards that you have pulled out over the past month, or even year, and then to note some of the patterns and even observe some of the themes that showed up in your readings based on what actually happened in your life.

This can be a lot of fun. It helps you to see how close you are to that higher self because you can actually see how things are working for you. There is no way you are going to be able to remember your draws from a year ago. But if you make some charts, you can look back and see these and how they work for you. All that you have to do with this is start with the daily pull that we talked about before, then get crafty about how you are going to write the information down.

You may find that working on a big chart with 10 columns on the top and every card of the tarot deck making rows on the side is a good place to start. Based on the card that you pull out each day, you will make it on the chart. After a few months or a year, you will be able to see which card you have pulled out when and more. This is a good way to see which themes are coming up on you throughout the year, and you will be able to work from there.

This is just one suggestion of what you may want to do when it comes to the tarot cards. You can definitely go through and mix it up or find another method that will make this work out better for your needs. But you will find that your own personal readings are going to become more profound if you are able to pull out the tarot cards and then track how they have worked throughout a few weeks and even longer!

Learn What the Card Wants You to Know

This is going to be similar to doing a tarot reading, but it is going to be done in reverse. Often, you already know what you are going to be laying out, the number of cards that are going to be there, and what each of the cards is going to symbolize for you. However, this kind of exercise that we are about to explore is going to turn this method around and will have you just lay out the number of cards that fits for you (sometimes this ends up being one, and maybe even twenty), to help you connect with your higher self, better than ever before.

To work with this one, you will need to cleanse out, shuffle, and vibe with the deck like you would with any other kind of reading. You can still ask the deck an overall question or feel certain energy when you are shuffling if you would like, but this is not necessary if you can't come up with a question or you just want to see where things go. The trick with this one is that you won't really know what you are pulling for until the card comes out.

With this one, you need to be very open, centered, and grounded when you decide to attempt this exercise because it is going to be a bit more difficult and advanced to do. And you want to be so open and grounded as you are doing it because this requires you to dig in deeper within yourself and within the cards once you are done with asking the question.

When you pull out each of the cards that you want, sit with it for a few moments, and just connect with that higher self before you decide to flip it over. You can then read the card and determine which part of your life, or even your question from the beginning, that this card is going to refer back to.

With this method, you are able to pull out as many cards from the deck as you would need. A good way to make this happen well is to try and take note of what the card is signifying as soon as you pick up on that information from your higher self. This way, when you finally are able to flip the card over, you are still going to remember what each one relates to in terms of your question. Go ahead and write some of the information down if you need. From this point, though, you are able to conduct the reading, as usual, to see how the question you asked has been answered.

Find a Study Buddy to Work with You

This may not seem like it is that helpful, but another person getting interested in the tarot and these kinds of readings with you means so much when you are a beginner in all of this. Whether you know someone who is already looking into tarot and who wants a friend as well, or you decide to pull one of your friends into this for the first time having a tarot "study buddy" can make a difference in the readings that you accomplish.

You will find that working in a group, whether it is with just one other person or you have a few, can be beneficial when it comes to referencing the tarot because the people in the group start to hold each other accountable. It also can instigate a fierce study of the cards. In addition, working with at least one other person will ensure that the information that you are looking at is going to be kept fresh, which helps you to understand more about the tarot cards and your readings faster than before.

If both of you are working with tarots and want to practice, this is the perfect opportunity. You can each sit down and practice some of the spreads that we talked about before to determine what is the right course of action for each of you. You can both learn something about the cards, help each other out if one gets stuck, and have some fun in the process.

You can also do some practicing with friends who may not be interested in doing these readings on their own, but who are willing to let you do a reading on them for practice. This can be a big scary along the way, but the more friends you are able to bring in, and the more spreads that you are able to practice, the better you are going to get with all of this.

Associate Your Own Chosen Keywords with Each of the Cards

This is another one of those exercises that are for the studious individuals who would really like to understand more about the meaning that is in their cards as quickly as possible. The gist of working with this exercise is to go through all of the cards in the deck, and then write down a few keywords with each of the cards to help you describe them or to help you remember them more.

Over time, you will be able to use your notebook of keywords when you are conducting your readings more than you use some of the information that we are talking about in this guidebook. Regardless of how you decide to use this, though, putting this massive store of information down into your own words, with just a few keywords with each card, will help you to learn more about the cards and how to use them.

For those who like to spend even more time studying and are ready for some extra work, you may find that doing the same exercise for the reversed meanings of the cards can help out as well. On the other hand, you could also split this up and do two keywords for what is called the standard placement of the card, and then have two keywords for the reversed placement of the card. However, you choose to make this happen—you will find that picking out your own keywords to describe the deck is going to really help you to understand the cards better and will ensure that you are able to really have some of the best readings of tarot possible.

Start Out with the Court Cards First

It is really easy to take a look at the tarot cards and feel overwhelmed by how many there are. This can make us want to take a step back because there is just so much information that we need to keep track of in a short amount of time, and trying to fit in all of that information, along with all of the spreads that we can try out, can seem like a monumental task.

This exercise is going to help out with this by cutting out some of the cards and allowing you to just work with a few of them at the time. You can basically take out any segment of the tarot deck that you would like, and then use that part to help with your reading rather than trying to memorize and work with all of the cards. It is often best to work with segments that are related, though. For example, with this one, you would only use the face or the court cards of the Minor Arcana.

When we look at the Minor Arcana, we see that there are 56 cards to work with rather than the 22 cards that are found in the Major Arcana. So even if you just work with the Minor Arcana, it can end up being a ton of cards that you need to focus on. This is why we are going to spend a moment slimming it down further and just working with the Kings Queens, Knights, Pages, and Aces and using these for some of the readings.

Readings of this nature, with fewer cards at hand, are going to be suited the best for any question that is about a big life event and queries about those people who are in your life. You are sure to get some answers that are really firm to the question, but you will find that you are able to learn more about these 20 cards in the tarot deck than you would if they were just 20 out of 56, or even 20 out of the whole deck of 78.

Try Doing the Readings with the Major Arcana Alone

This one is similar to the ideas that we talked about above. This one is going to focus on reading your fortune, or the fortune of your querent, using just the 22 cards that are found in the Major Arcana. These cards are going to demonstrate the major events that can happen in your lifetime, so questions that work the best for this kind of reading will be related to the flavor of one's life direction, what stage of life you are dealing with, and what your overall goals in this life should be.

As you can see here, there are a lot of different exercises that you can use that are going to make your life with the tarot cards a bit easier. You can choose how much or how little you would like to do with them. But for those who really want to catch on to the meaning of the tarot cards quickly, and who are interested in really being able to do well, these exercises are going to provide you with the help and assistance that you really need.

Chapter 10: The Danger of Tarot – Things to Know About Misusing Tarot

There are a lot of people who are a bit worried about getting into the tarot readings. They worry that they are doing something that is dangerous or that is going to cause them and the other person in the reading some harm. They feel that they are lifting up the veil between the spiritual and the physical world. And when they do this, they worry that they are going to let in not only the good energies and the good spirits but the negative ones as well.

However, this brings up the question about whether this risk is something that can come into your life or if it is really that bad. There can be a danger that comes with using these cards, but it is not going to be the danger that you think. When you work with the tarot cards, there is not going to be a kind of demonic force that will descend on you if you decide to open up the cards. This doesn't mean, though, that there isn't a dark side that comes with the tarot either.

The biggest thing to worry about here is that the purpose of the tarot is going to be misconstrued and it is going to get itself lumped together with séances, Ouija boards, and other things that you may have a negative connotation with as well. But the tarot cards are not used as a tool to summon spirits or to talk to the dead. Instead, it is a tool that is used to help you explore yourself.

The tarot cards are much different compared to what some of the other options are going to be. Those are going to focus on the spirit world a lot, and will sometimes invite spirits and other bad things into your life. This is why there is a lot of negatives that come with this kind of stuff, and most people are advised not to use these at all.

However, when we are looking at the tarot cards, we are looking at something that is different. You do want to connect to your higher self, but this is a part of you. This is not a part of the spirit world. It is a part of yourself, something that all of us have, whether we choose to recognize it or not. This makes it a good thing, not something that is in the spirit world and will cause us any issues.

Tarot cards are not going to predict things that are way in the future or rely on a spirit to tell us something. It can make a prediction about what we have done in the past and in the present, and maybe for a short time in the future. But all of this is going to be based on what we are dealing with now, and it is often going to rely on the intuition that we have inside of all of us. This makes it safe to use and can be a fun way to learn more about yourself, no danger or spirits required.

Taking Some Cautionary Measures

With the above in mind, along with some of the other things that we have talked about in this guidebook, it is important to make sure that you take a few cautionary measures. The tarot card readings are very safe and good for you to use, but you may want to take some time to cleanse and protect yourself energetically before you really dive into doing any of your readings. This isn't necessarily done to keep the evil spirits away. But it is going to make sure that you are keeping any negative expectations and energy away so that they don't mess with the readings that you are having along the way.

There are a lot of people reading tarot cards, who will put a lot of importance of cleansing their deck before a reading. While this is something that you can consider doing, sometimes it is more important to make sure that you, including your body and your own mind, is cleaned out before you start out.

If you come to a reading for the cards feeling anxious, down, nervous, tired, or any other negative emotion, it is going to really affect the cards that you choose to go with, and it can change up the way that you choose to interpret them. Think of this as an important date that you are dealing with. You wouldn't show up to a big interview or to a date looking cranky, smelly, and more. So don't show up to your tarot reading being this way either. You want to bring the positive energy, and your best self to the mix to see the results.

The good news is that there are a few different ways that you are able to cleanse up yourself energetically before you decide to do your tarot readings. These work, whether you are doing the readings on yourself or on another person. Some of the best ways to make sure that you are cleansed out energetically before starting a new tarot reading is going to include:

1. Take a nice long and hot bath or shower. You can add in some Epsom salts and even a few essential oils. The best ones to include in the bath will be sage, rosemary, and lavender. While you are in the bath, try just to sit back and enjoy it. See if you can clear the mind and think about absolutely nothing while you are doing it.
2. Spend about ten minutes doing some kind of meditation. A good way to do this is just to spend some time observing your breath. Imagine that you are exhaling away any of the expectations and stress in the body, and inhaling a light that is white and pure one that is able to cleanse out all of the cells of the body.

3. Exercise and dance. If you have enough time to do this, consider doing some movement before you do a reading. This is very powerful and is one of the most effective ways to move energy back into your body while kicking some of the bad stuff away from you.
4. Listen to some Gregorian chants, some soft and rhythmic drums or another similar kind of music. Sit in the silence and light a few candles while burning some incense to help you become more centered. This only needs to happen for a few minutes before doing the reading.
5. Light a big stick of dried sage and waft the smoke all around your body to cleanse you.

You can do all of these, or just a few of the ones that you think will be the most effective at helping you to cleanse out the energy that is in your body. If you come in with a lot of negativity in your thoughts, or there are any negative emotions that are hanging around, then it is going to be much harder to get some of the readings that you want, and you, or your client, is going to be a bit disappointed in that.

Cleansing Your Deck

We mentioned above how some of those who do tarot readings feel strongly about doing a cleanse over the deck before they decide to use them. This is not always necessary, but it is something to consider if someone else has used the deck since your last reading. Some readers of the tarot cards believe that these cards are capable of absorbing the energy that is around them. And with this in mind, if you do not cleanse the deck before each reading, it is likely that the reading is not going to be that accurate.

Whether you believe that this is going to be a problem with your readings or not, it is still a nice thing to do on occasion. It can help you to get into the mindset that you need for reading, and you will be more prepared for what you are about to do. Some of the simple steps that you are able to follow in order to get the deck you are using for this reading ready will include:

1. Take the deck and knock on it one time. When that is done, waft your hand over it, just like you are pushing away a bad smell or something that is on top of it.
2. Sometimes, just being able to take the deck and shuffle it around is enough to break up some of the stagnant energy that is in it. Whether you do a cleanse of the deck or not, doing this shuffling is a good way to move the cards around and can change up the reading that you are about to do.
3. Some people believe very strongly in the energy of the moon and the light that it has to offer. If you do, then you may want to place your deck in a location where

the moonlight is able to touch it overnight to give it a new sense of energy.
4. Crystals can be a good way to cleanse out the deck as well. Put your deck into a bag of quartz crystals and then let it sit for a few hours or even overnight before you decide to use them.
5. Some people like to waft some smoke, especially sage smoke, all over the cards. This is going to be kind of smelly and smoky but is a great way to clean out the energy that is in the cards while also helping you to cleanse your own thoughts and the energy in the room.

When you are doing some of these readings, it is important for you to remember that intention is very critical. This is true no matter what kind of spiritual or metaphysical work you are doing along the way. The kind of intention that you are doing will dictate the kind of energy or the kind of vibe that you are putting out to the world, and this is going to make a difference in the experience that you are going to have during that reading.

First, before you even start with a whole new reading, it is important to set up some clear intentions before you get started. Think about some of the reasons that you are doing this reading. What are you hoping to gain from this reading, or what is the querent hoping to gain from the reading? Make sure that the intentions that you have at this time are pure and that no negative or creepy thoughts start to make their way into the mix.

Let's take a look at an example of what an impure or a creepy intention with these cards would be like. A good example of this would be, "I intend to use my tarot cards to read my ex-boyfriend's mind and find out if he was banging that waitress." If you find that you are struggling with the relationship of the past and you would like to get some help from these cards, then you need to go with an intention that is more positive. A good positive intention to work with on the case above would be something like, "I intend to get some new ideas for how I can move on from my past relationship."

These are two different statements or questions that you are able to ask, but they are going to give quite different answers. And the second one is one that is actually going to help you out with getting over the issue and feeling so much better. The tarot cards are probably not going to let you know if your ex was cheating on you with the waitress. And even if they did, that would not help you feel better or get over the relationship any easier.

But if you ask the tarot cards some of the steps that you are able to take in order to get over the relationship in a healthy manner, in one that can help you and actually make you feel happier, then this is going to be productive. The tarot cards can help to point you in the right direction for this kind of thing, and the answers are going to make you feel a million times better, especially since you now have a clear path to follow to make it happen.

Even as a beginner, your readings are going to turn out so much better both the personal ones and the ones that you do for other people, if you are able to keep your intentions pure. If you feel like your client is starting to veer off with some bad intentions, or ones that won't work so well, this could lead to a bad reading. Try to steer them back with some good suggestions of intentions that are much better so that they can get the answers that they truly need with their tarot reading.

The Real Danger of These Cards

Now, we are going to get down to some of the nitty gritty when it comes with this. There can be a danger that comes with these cards, but it is often not the same danger that others may tell you about or that you have heard about in the past. The biggest risk that is going to come from these tarot cards is if you make a big misunderstanding about what they say, or you decide to take the readings too seriously.

This is not to say that you should just mess around and joke about the cards. This is something that can lead you on a journey about yourself, knowing more about who you are as a person in a way that you may not have been able to do in the past or through other methods. But if you take it too seriously, you are missing out on some of the fun learning process, and some of the passion that should come with these cards.

If you are a beginner, and you haven't been able to take the time to understand the meanings of the card fully, and the fact that each card is going to have more than one meaning, it is possible that you are going to get something like the Death card in one of your readings and then assume that this literally means Death. Or you could get the Tower card and assume that it spells out disaster.

While we spent some time before looking at the different meanings of the cards and how they mean different things based on what is near them and what direction they are in, for someone who is a beginner, pulling out one of those two cards, or both, may seem a bit frightening and could be enough to taint the experience that you are having with the tarot reading.

If you are prone to taking the reading really seriously, then the Death or the Tower card is going to seem all that more frightening than before. The readings that you are able to get with the tarot cards can be really illuminating, and you will be amazed at all of the fascinating things that you are able to learn from them. But remember that they are not the last word. And these cards rarely mean as bad of a thing as we build up in our mind.

The point here is that your tarot reading is supposed to help you to search into yourself and learn more in the process. This kind of reading is not meant to be obsessively believed, but rather, it is something that you need to contemplate and learn more about.

One thing that you may notice when you start to work with other people on these readings is how they hang onto all of the things you say like it is the end all of everything. They will believe each word you say, without questioning it or really understanding what is going on. It is so important to question your tarot readings and make sure that you, or your querent, is asking the right questions.

Think of the cards of the tarot as a good friend of yours. These cards, just like a good friend, will give you some advice—whether you choose to ask for it or not. Do you always take the advice that your friends give? Of course not, especially if it is really bad advice. Often there is going to be some opinion, fear, or bias of the friend when they give the advice, and that is why you may listen to them, and then determine for yourself if you are going to follow that advice or not.

This is the same idea that you are able to work with when you are doing your tarot readings. The questions that you ask and the intent that you get from them as you read is going to be different in each scenario. And just because the cards seem to point to one side or one piece of advice does not mean that you should follow them with a blind level of faith.

This is something that you are going to learn how to do better with time. But if you are just blindly following the advice without really learning about them, then some of the readings are going to be very frightening and probably will change the experience that you have with the client as well.

Stick with What You Know

It is tempting as a beginner to want to show off to the client and really show them all of the cool things that you know. You want to be able to do some more complex spreads and show them all of the different things that you are able to do with them. But if you are truly a beginner and are just learning how to work with the cards and learning what their meanings are, then this is probably not the best thing to work with.

It is best, even if you are just starting and your knowledge base is not that big, to just start with what you know. As we discussed above, there are some people who are going to come to your readings and will take every word that you say as the absolute truth. If you give them some bad advice in the hopes of impressing them, without knowing them or reading the cards in the proper manner, then this could end up very badly for you and for the other person.

Be honest with your client. Tell them if you are just starting out and that the two of you are on a journey together to learn more. Let them know that you are excited to be able to read their cards, but that you are just learning the meanings and will make the information available to the best of your abilities. Being open about this, and letting them know when something seems like it doesn't make sense to you and when you need to redo some things will help the reading to go more smoothly. Don't try to lie to your clients or make a bunch of stuff up in the hopes of impressing the and really giving them bad advice or making them not want to come back and work with you again.

Often the dangers that are associated with the tarot cards are there because more people don't understand how these are supposed to work. They assume that these cards are going to be the same thing as some of the other psychic options, and they worry about some of the negative spirits and energies that they are going to be inviting in.

The secret here is that the tarot cards are going to be different than all of these. You are relying on yourself, even a higher self, but still you in the process, and you are relying on your intuition. There is no summoning of spirits or working with the other world to get the readings done. And that is why, for the most part, you will find that doing a tarot reading is a very safe process to work with.

Chapter 11: Tips for the Beginner of Tarot Cards

Now that we have spent some time learning more about the tarot cards, how to work on a few spreads, how to read the different cards, and more, it is time to look at a few tips that will make this whole process a bit easier to work with.

As you have gone through this guidebook, it is likely that you see all of this information and feel a bit overwhelmed about it all. That is perfectly normal. This may have been a topic that you didn't know all that much about in the beginning—and now, you are trying to learn about 78 cards, plus their reversals, a bunch of spreads, and how to connect with the higher power that is found within yourself. It is perfectly normal to be a bit confused and to wonder how you are going to be able to put it all together.

That is where this chapter is going to come into play. We are going to take a look at some of the tips that you need to follow in order to get started with the tarot cards and get the most out of the readings that you are going to be doing. Some of the tips that you can follow as a beginner of tarot card readings will include:

Don't Try to Overreach in the Beginning

If you are going through the tarot cards and trying to learn it all, but you feel overwhelmed with it all, try not to panic and don't use this as an excuse to give up. These cards are going to demonstrate a powerful and energetic type of power, and they are going to teach us so much. And for some of us, this is going to seem really overwhelming. But because of the value that we are able to get from these cards, it really would be a shame if you just give up because there seems to be too much information to remember!

Remind yourself that these tarot cards are supposed to be fun as well! Yes, they are serious and can help us with divination, but if you are not enjoying the readings that you do at all, then you are not going through these the right way. Maybe the problem is that you are trying to take on too much in the beginning. Starting out with simple reading, or going through with some of the brain exercises that we talked about a few chapters back can help you to reduce your worry and can make it much easier for you to learn how these work.

For those who are not necessarily feeling overwhelmed by the tarot, but are trying to do too much, consider something new. Maybe you are doing a lot with the cards, but do you really know these cards yet? Do you actually remember any of the spreads that you have gone through and worked with, and are you starting to remember any of the particular cards and their meanings?

The goal of those questions is to get a firm "yes." If you are not able to answer in this manner, then it is time to re-simplify and rescale things to make them more manageable. This is not a bad thing. Each person is going to learn how to do these tarot readings on their own time, and if you need more time to connect with your higher self and to learn more along the way, then that is just fine.

Consider Keeping a Tarot Journal

Anyone who spends time reading these tarot cards will find that it is really beneficial to keep a tarot journal. You don't even need to work with a physical notebook since you can work with other options such as your phone. Note what cards tend to appear on a regular basis, and even which of the cards in the deck you are drawn to the most often. Note how you feel about the readings, how accurate they are, and how you intend to proceed now that you have seen the cards.

This may seem like a lot of work, but it is going to make a difference in how well you are able to connect to the cards. And it isn't something that you have to do each time that you complete your reading if that seems to be too much for you.

The more that you are able to process this kind of information about the readings, though, the better you will become at integrating the learning experiences into your life. At least try to write down what seems like the most important information after each reading.

In whatever method seems to work the best for you, start to record these experiences of tarot, the readings, and some of the more intense pulls of the cards. Over time, and maybe with a look through your notes, you are going to start seeing a nice pattern between the cards that you pull and the events that happen in your life. Sometimes, there is even a connection with the emotional moments that happen in your life.

Along the way, you may notice that your intuition and psychic powers are growing. You should take note of these as well because this will show that you are really learning the tarot cards and that you are going to get better over time. Embrace the change that these tarot readings offer by keeping a record of all the realizations that you have that are life-altering.

In time, you are going to be better at this. You will learn what works for you, and even without the journaling and the notes, you will be able to see that the tarot cards are good at explaining the life events that have happened are happening—and will happen—in your life. Over time, you are going to become a tarot expert, and keeping this journal is really going to help.

Always Remember Who Is in Charge

This is something that can be hard for a lot of us to imagine, but when you are doing the tarot reading, even if you are working with someone else who asked the question, you are the one who is really the star. Your higher self is going to connect with you through the pictures on the cards, and it is that connection that will allow you to answer these questions in a truthful manner while providing the answers that you or your querent are going to ask.

You are always the one in charge. The cards are being directed by you, even if you are not able to see that right away. And if you start to feel a bit frustrated or overwhelmed by the tarot, don't let the anger that you are feeling here get in the way of the readings that you do. No matter how much anger and frustration is there, you are the one in charge, so it is not the fault of the cards. You are still learning, though, and this is absolutely okay. Allow yourself to show some patients, learn how to forgive and move on, and allow yourself to be the one in charge of the whole experience.

If you feel frustrated because you aren't really understanding the message that the cards are starting to show you or tell you, then remember there is nothing wrong with the cards. It is something that is wrong with you. Maybe right at this moment, for some reason, you are not open to receiving the messages that the cards are sending out to you. This is not a sign that the cards are of bad quality or worthless and they are not wrong here.

Any time that this kind of frustration shows up, just remember that the power of the tarot is going to lie within your own soul. You need to open yourself up to the message that comes up, and maybe, after a break, you will come again to the spread and approach it with a more open mind.

Keep It Simple

Sometimes, it is really easy to look at all of the information and all of the cards and feel like you are going to get really lost in the system that makes up these cards. But if you try to learn all of the systems, all of the spreads, and more at once, then you will feel overwhelmed and will want to give it all up.

Instead of trying to take it all in at once, make a commitment to yourself to really keep things as simple as possible. There is a lot to learn with the tarot, and it is not a good idea to try and learn it all at once. This is a process and a journey. And it is fine if you don't try to learn it all overnight. You don't even need to know it all before you undergo your first reading experience!

A better option to help you get the most done with all of this is to stick with things that are as simple as possible. This means that you have to stick with a few simple techniques, the basic meanings of the cards, and the easiest spreads—probably a few of each, to help you out. As you spend more time learning about the tarot cards and more, you will find that you can take on more information and enhance your readings in that manner.

Find a Way to Create a Personal Connection to the Cards

Many beginners take all of the work with the tarot cards too literally. They grab some information about it and try to memorize the meanings of the cards and all of the spreads. They think that this is the best way for them to do their readings, but in reality, they are holding themselves back if they concentrate too much on the book work and not on their own personal connection with the tarot cards that are before them. If you do not have an intuitive connection with the cards, and you are not able to work with your higher self, then it is hard to get the deep and meaningful relationship that you want, and the good readings of the cards in the process.

When you start to relate to these cards on a personal level, you will find that some of the intuitive insights that you need with these readings, the insights that your querents are looking for as well, are going to start taking off. There are several ways that you are able to do this. First, look to your everyday life to find some personal examples of these cards working for you. Think about what card is describing your day or your week? What card is going to start representing your best friend, your parent, and more?

Learn How to Reach Your Higher Self

If you are struggling with reaching your higher self or at least struggling with listening to that higher self, then it is going to be tough to go with the tarot readings. The higher self is going to ensure that you are able to shuffle the cards in the right way, cleanse them in the right way, and pull them out with a good interpretation in order to see results with your readings.

Those who don't really believe in the higher self or who won't take the time to develop this kind of thing will find that doing a tarot reading is really hard for them to do. This is because you are not going to get good readings without trusting in your higher self. Learning the best ways to develop it, which starts with just believing in the higher self, and you will be amazed at how well you can do some of these different readings.

It is fine if you struggle with this a little bit in the beginning. It is possible that you are not going to start out with a strong connection with your higher self. And this is perfectly fine. Being open to what your higher self is telling you, and spending some time learning the cards and trusting your intuition will make this happen. It will take some time, and it is not going to be something that is instant for you. But it is something that you can learn how to develop if you just believe in it and work on it for the long term.

Swap Out for a Simple Spread

There are a lot of beginners who like to really go hard on some of the spreads that they are doing for the querents or for themselves. They think that these complicated spreads are going to help you to really see the results that you need, and will really impress the querents that you work with. But sometimes, working with something that is a bit easier, and doesn't have the complications, can make a big difference.

Nearly every beginner book talking about tarot is going to include the Celtic tarot spread. We even spent some time talking about it. It is a beautiful spread, but with ten cards to make it happen, it is not always the best place to start for the Tarot beginner.

Instead of using this complicated of a spread, consider going with a spread that is a little bit easier. You may find that doing a simple spread that is between one to three cards, and no more than five, will be a lot easier. It may seem like you are going backward and not going to get the good readings that you want, but you will be surprised at how much insight you are able to get from a reading that is only one card.

Read the Picture That Is on Your Card

One of the easiest ways for a beginner to start to understand more about what the card in the tarot is meaning is to look at the picture. There are some beautiful drawings that are on these cards, and taking the time to read through them is going to be important when you want to get an accurate reading for yourself or for another person. Take some time to look at the picture that is on your card and figure out what is happening, why that situation is happening, and even the moral of the story.

Then, after you have done this kind of analysis, you can relate it back to what you are currently experiencing in your life. What can the story that is on the card tell you about the life you are in right now. And are there some new lessons that you are able to learn from that card as well.

The best thing about working with this kind of technique is that you won't have to spend a lot of time memorizing the meanings that come with the card. You can simply look at the picture that is on the card and use that as the way that you figure out the meaning of the card. This technique is going to be so powerful that you could spend your whole readings doing this.

Tune into What Your Intuition Is Telling You

The neat thing that comes with the tarot cards is that it is all about your own intuition and what you are able to get out of the readings when you focus on that instead of anything else. It doesn't really matter what the meaning of your cards says, or what we have said with this guidebook. If your intuition is leading you a different way with the cards that you pull and the information that comes with it, you will need to go with that.

If you feel that your readings are not going the way that you would like, it is time to put down the books and take in the energy of the Tarot card that is right in front of you. Focus on the here and now and nothing else. It doesn't matter if you are looking at the card and you connect with a different meaning that what you find online or in a book.

When this happens, we often feel confused, or we think that we are reading the deck in the wrong way. But the truth is that if we are doing the readings in the proper manner, and we are focusing on what our higher self is saying, then this is going to happen sometimes. When your intuition reads the card in a different way, this is such a powerful thing, and you should definitely follow it and see where it takes you.

Perform Some Tarot Readings for Yourself

Ignore anyone who ends up telling you that it is a bad idea to read tarot on yourself. How are you supposed to learn how all of this comes together and how to do a good reading if the very first time you do one is on someone else? Most tarot readers who are successful with what they are trying to do here will find that doing some readings on themselves can make a world of difference in the amount of success that they can find.

Doing tarot is going to be such a powerful tool when it comes to your own self-discovery and your personal development, so why not do readings on yourself and make use of all the benefits that come with it. In fact, when you are starting out and doing some of your own tarot readings, you are the number one best client to work with.

As a beginner, you should stop and make a bit of time each day to do your own readings of the tarot readings. Even if you are just doing a few cards each day, it is a great way to get used to this whole process and to get in touch with your own intuition. The more that you can do this, the better you will get. And this makes you the perfect candidate to do the work when it is time to bring someone else into the mix.

Forget About the Rules for a Little Bit

Many beginners want to know all of the rules that come with the tarot. They will find someone who knows about tarot and who has been doing the readings for some time, and they want to ask a bunch of questions about what is allowed and what is not allowed. They will ask whether someone else can touch their cards if they can split up the deck and only work with small parts of it, and more.

Each person is going to follow their tarot reading in a different manner. You don't have any set rules that you have to follow. Outside of doing some practice and learning how to work with your intuition, there are no hard set rules that you have to stick with when it comes to this. Learn a bit about the cards so that you can get started, learn about your intuition, and remain ethical with the readings that you do, and you are doing the tarot the right way.

Find Out What These Cards All Mean to You

One of the best exercises that you are able to focus on when it comes to working in tarot as a beginner is going to ask yourself the question, "How does Tarot work?" By reflecting on these questions and coming up with the answer that is the best for you, you will find that it is easier to get a sense of what these cards mean to you, and the best way that you are able to work with these tools.

Now, you will find that with each reader, and even with each querent, the answer to this one is going to change. And that is normal. You may see that these cards are going to be more of a predictive tool, a coaching tool, or even something that is fun and can impress your friends and family.

Once you know what these cards mean to you, write it out, post it on a blog or on the computer, and say it out loud. You need to have a firm meaning of what these cards are going to do in your life. This will help you to really work hard on coming up with the right answers that you need, and ensuring that you learn the right way to do this based on what you are hoping to get out of it.

Use the Tarot in a Mindful Manner

One of the biggest mistakes that you may make as a beginner to tarot reading is that you start to ask the same question over and over again. They do this in the hopes that they are going to get a better answer when they do it again. Or they will do a reading when they are really emotional or when they are going to shut down instead of receiving the right insight for their needs.

This is not how the tarot is meant to work. You can't redo it in the hopes of getting better results. You need to ask the question, and then accept the results that you are getting. You are not always going to get the happy go lucky answers that you would like. Sometimes, the answers are going to be good, and sometimes, they may warn you that things are not going to work out the best for you. This is just something that you need to be aware of, and you need just to accept the answers that you are going to need.

Instead of doing the process over and over again, you need to be willing to use the tarot cards in a mindful manner. Draw on the cards any time that you can ensure that your mind is open and the heart is open. Treat both the cards and yourself with the respect that you need, and accept the wisdom that these cards are going to offer to you.

Learning how to work with the tarot cards is a great way to learn more about yourself, about your world, and so much more—and when you take some time to follow the tips above, you are going to go from beginner to expert level with tarot card readings in no time at all!

Conclusion

Thank you for making it through to the end of *Tarot for Beginners*! Let's hope it was informative and able to provide you with all of the tools you need to achieve your goals—whatever they may be.

The next step is to start working on your own tarot readings. This is all about learning what the cards mean, how to use them, and becoming one with your own spiritual power. It takes some time, and a new connection that you need to work with, but the results are going to be amazing overall.

This guidebook has taken some time to explore the tarot cards that you can use and how to make the most out of your first reading. From learning about the history of the tarot cards and how they first started out to what the different cards mean and even some of the spreads that you are able to use, this guidebook will help you to become an expert at reading the tarot cards in no time.

When you are ready to start doing some of your very own tarot card readings but are not sure where you should start, make sure to check out this guidebook to help you get started!

www.ingramcontent.com/pod-product-compliance
Lightning Source LLC
Chambersburg PA
CBHW071353080526
44587CB00017B/3085